MORE TRUE MYSTERIES

Unsolved mysteries have a fascination for most people—especially unsolved *true* mysteries. Fitting the facts together is like making up a jigsaw puzzle. With thought and patience, it seems, *a* solution can be arrived at. But the trouble with true mysteries is that you can never be certain that you have all the pieces . . .

3 bcd

More True Mysteries

Bob Hoare

Illustrations by John Hutchinson

CAROUSEL EDITOR: ANNE WOOD

CAROUSEL BOOKS
A DIVISION OF TRANSWORLD PUBLISHERS LTD

MORE TRUE MYSTERIES

A CAROUSEL BOOK 0 552 54048 X

First publication in Great Britain

PRINTING HISTORY

Carousel edition published 1974

Text Copyright © Bob Hoare 1974
Illustrations Copyright © Transworld Publishers Ltd. 1974

This book is set in Baskerville 12/12½ pt.

Carousel Books are published by Transworld Publishers Ltd.,
Cavendish House, 57–59 Uxbridge Road, Ealing, London W.5

Made and printed in Great Britain by
Richard Clay (The Chaucer Press), Ltd., Bungay, Suffolk.

**NOTE: The Australian price appearing on the
back cover is the recommended retail price.**

MORE TRUE MYSTERIES

INTRODUCTION

UNSOLVED MYSTERIES HAVE a fascination for most people—especially unsolved true mysteries. As letters from readers of my earlier book, *True Mysteries*, indicate, there is a temptation to study the facts and work out your own solution.

This new book contains ten true mysteries, some from the past, some from modern times. Nine of them remain unsolved although, in some cases, solutions have been put forward. That is one of the tantalising things about a true mystery. Fitting the facts together is like making up a jigsaw puzzle. With thought and patience, it seems, the solution can be arrived at. But the trouble with true mysteries is that you can never be certain that you have all the pieces.

However, a vital missing piece might turn up at any time no matter how old a mystery is. Most people assumed that no one would ever know what happened to Salomon Andrée who vanished in his balloon over the Arctic. Yet thirty-three years later his body was found and a diary telling almost the whole story. Is it impossible that Colonel Fawcett's fate might become known by a similar discovery?

The Fawcett mystery and others in the present volume, those from the past as well as those from modern times, could still be solved one day. In the meantime, consider the facts that we have ... and wonder.

BOB HOARE

"Karina",
Wells Lane,
Ascot,
Berks.

THE MYSTERY OF STONEHENGE

STONEHENGE STANDS ON Salisbury Plain in Wiltshire, eight miles north of Salisbury and two miles west of Amesbury. It is a great circle of huge stone pillars. Some are upright. Others are lying on the ground where they fell centuries ago.

Every year, one quarter of a million people from all over the world visit the site. They marvel at the skill with which, long, long ago, early men raised the immense pillars. They wonder where the stones come from, how they were transported, how they were put up. They wonder most of all over Stonehenge's biggest mystery. Why was this monument built?

Visitors to that lonely place must have done the same for over two thousand years, and the mystery of Stonehenge is known to have fascinated people for centuries.

Once it was believed to be a temple built by the wizard of the Dark Ages, Merlin, in memory of warriors killed in battle against invaders. Merlin and Stonehenge were linked by Geoffrey of Monmouth writing in the twelfth century. Yet Geoffrey did not suggest that Merlin made the monument by magic. According to him, Merlin had the stones transported to Stonehenge by manual labour and the monument built the same way. This probably shows that people in Geoffrey's day had had handed down to them vague accounts of the building of Stonehenge.

In the seventeenth century, King Charles II asked a

scholar named John Aubrey to make a study of Stonehenge. He inspected the remains carefully and came to the conclusion that Stonehenge had been a pagan temple. Aubrey admitted that he was 'groping in the dark' but he said it was possible that the temple belonged to the Druids.

For a long time afterwards, this story was widely believed. But we know that, about this, Aubrey was hopelessly wrong. The druids were priests and teachers of the Celtic tribes. They lived in England long after the time when Stonehenge was built. For we know, today, when that was. Over many years archaeologists have studied Stonehenge and solved some of the monument's mysteries.

These experts have worked out exactly what Stonehenge used to look like. Indeed, they know, from the evidence they have found, that the monument was produced as a result of three different periods of building. It existed in three different forms—Stonehenge 1, Stonehenge 2 and Stonehenge 3.

Stonehenge 1 was built about 2200 B.C., in the New Stone Age. It consisted of a large, circular space about one hundred yards across. Around it were a bank and a ditch.

In one place the ground was left level to form the entrance. On either side of this there was probably a stone and, some distance outside the circle, stood another stone now called the Heel Stone. It was given this name by John Aubrey. He said he had seen in it the imprint of a 'friar's heel'.

This seems to be a reference by Aubrey to a legend connected with Stonehenge and this particular stone. According to the legend, a friar living near Salisbury once made the Devil angry, and he picked up a huge block of stone and hurled it at the holy man. The stone struck the friar on the heel but he was so strong or protected by holiness that the stone did not hurt him.

What happened was that his heel made an imprint in the stone.

The Heel Stone rises sixteen feet above the ground with four underground. It is eight feet wide and six feet thick and it weighs thirty-five tons.

The ditch was about twenty feet wide and six feet deep. It had steep sides and a flat bottom. The bank was inside the ditch, and on its inner edge there was a ring of fifty-six pits about four feet wide and three feet deep. No one knows what these pits were for. They were first noted by John Aubrey and they are now called the Aubrey Holes. About half of them are marked with white spots and they can be plainly seen in the short grass.

Stonehenge 2 was probably built about 1700–1600 B.C. The builders are thought to have been the Beaker people. They had come to Britain a little earlier from across the North Sea. They are called the Beaker people because stone beakers are found in their graves.

The Beaker people widened the entrance to the circle by filling in the ditch with earth from the mound. Then they made an avenue from Stonehenge to the River Avon two miles away, marking it out with a ditch and a mound on either side. Between the circle and the Heel Stone on the avenue they put up two tall stones.

In the circle they began to set up two circles of pillars made from huge bluestones, one circle six feet inside the other. Extra stones were placed inside these unfinished circles in line with the entrance. Then, for an unknown reason, all these stones were taken down.

Stonehenge 3 was started about 1600 B.C. at the beginning of the Bronze Age in Britain. A series of massive stones weighing upwards of twenty-five tons each were raised in a horseshoe pattern. Linking each pair of stones was a massive stone lintel. These lintels are thought to have given Stonehenge its name for the name means 'the hanging stones'.

Outside the horseshoe was raised a ring of the same stones and the ring was closed with a series of lintels. Later the bluestones of Stonehenge 2 were used again. They were carefully shaped and then set up to form an oval inside the horseshoe.

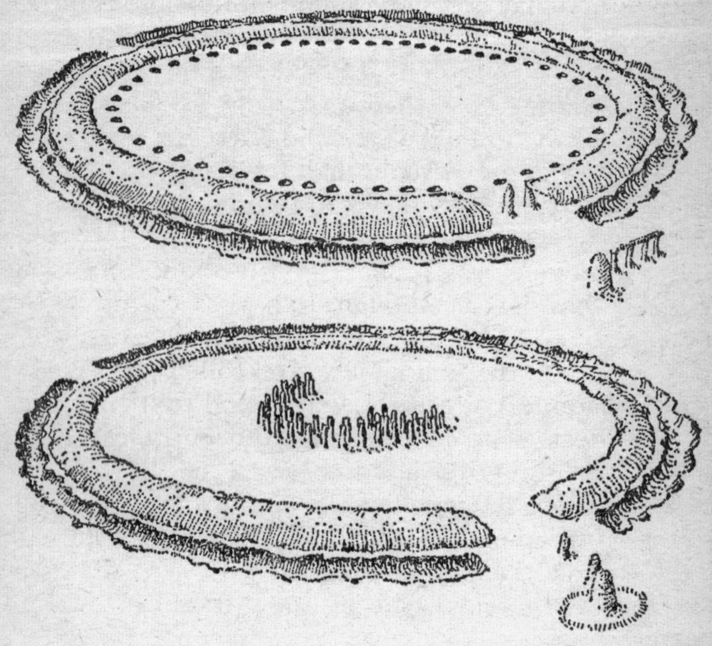

Afterwards the builders dug holes outside the main circle. Archaeologists believe that they were going to put up more bluestones there but this was not done. For some reason, the builders appear to have changed their minds. They pulled down the bluestones in the middle and rearranged them in a new pattern. This took the form of a circle within the main circle, and a horseshoe within the horseshoe.

Stonehenge 3 was probably finished about 1300 B.C. and the picture opposite shows what it is believed to have looked like.

The whole project, from the start of Stonehenge 1 to the finish of Stonehenge 3, probably took over nine hundred years. The amount of work done in all the building is staggering. It has been worked out that it took more than one and a half million man-hours of work. That is equal to forty men working for twenty-four hours a day non-stop for one hundred years!

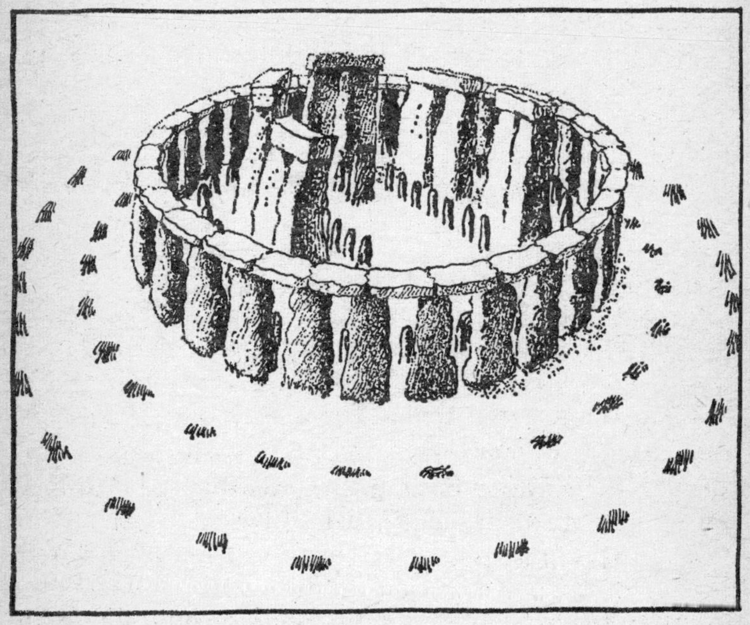

A professor in astronomy, Gerald S. Hawkins, said: 'The cost of building Stonehenge to the people who built it must have been equal, at least, to the cost of the United States Space Programme. It might have meant much more to the people who built it.'

The ditches and pits and holes for the stones were dug with pick-axes made from the antlers of deer. The ground in the area is chalky, and the broken chalk was scraped together and shovelled into baskets with the shoulder-blades of cattle. Then the baskets were carried to wherever the chalk was required.

In modern times, archaeologists have carried out experiments with the same kind of tools, showing exactly how the work was done. They have also done the same work using steel picks and shovels and buckets and found out an interesting fact. This modern equipment only allowed the work to be done in half the time. In other words, the prehistoric tools were remarkably efficient.

The massive stones used in building Stonehenge were not found nearby. Bringing them to Stonehenge was a difficult job for the builders.

The bluestones were brought all the way from the Prescelly Mountains in Pembrokeshire (Wales) and transporting them was one of the most remarkable engineering jobs done by prehistoric man in Europe. The Prescelly Mountains are one hundred and forty miles from Stonehenge as the crow flies. The stones —eighty of them weighing, in all, one hundred tons— were moved much more than that distance.

Scholars believe that the stones were moved most of the way by water. The stones would be pulled on sledges from the mountains to the bay at Milford Haven. Possibly the sledges would be helped along by tree trunks being placed under them. The Stone Age builders had not yet discovered the wheel.

From Milford Haven the bluestones would be taken on rafts by sea through the Bristol Channel and up the broad estuary of the River Severn to the River Avon. There each stone would be transferred to boats made from dug-out canoes lashed together side by side with a wooden platform on top to carry the stone. These boats would ride the narrow waters of the river much better than the clumsy rafts.

The boats might be pulled by a line from the shore or poled upriver. They would go nearly as far as the modern town of Bradford-on-Avon and then up the

River Frome almost to the present-day Frome. Here they would be landed and pulled by sledge about six miles to present-day Warminster. There they would again be loaded on to boats. They would float down the River Wylye to Wilton and eventually up the Salisbury Avon to the end of Stonehenge Avenue.

The total distance of this journey is about two hundred and forty miles, and nine-tenths of it are by water.

In 1954, an experiment was carried out to show how the bluestones probably reached Stonehenge. A copy of a bluestone was placed on a platform fastened to three dug-out canoes lashed together, and four boys poled this up the Salisbury Avon. At the same time, a bluestone was placed on a sledge and pulled over rough ground. It needed fourteen strong boys to do this.

The other stones in the monument came from Marlborough Downs in North Wiltshire, about twenty miles from Stonehenge. Some of these stones weigh about fifty tons, and they had to be hauled overland all the way.

Archaeologists have traced the probable route of these stones. They estimate that at least fifty men would be needed to pull one over the rough ground lashed to a huge sledge, and possibly as many as two hundred and fifty on one steep slope on the journey. Probably tree trunks were used as rollers under these sledges. Eight or ten rollers would be used and six men would be working on each, carrying it from the back to the front as it rolled out under the sledge.

The ropes used to pull the sledge and lash the stone to it were probably made of cow-hair or strips of leather plaited together.

There were thirty massive uprights in the outer ring in Stonehenge 3 and ten more in the horseshoe. Moving these and the great lintels must have taken many years.

All the stones used in Stonehenge 3 were shaped by

human efforts. To do this, smaller and perhaps harder stones may have been used. The building stones would be bashed and chipped and possibly rubbed with these smaller stones. Perhaps lines were first scraped on the building stone to show where a break was wanted. Stones may have been split down cracks with stone or wooden wedges. To work each stone probably took several months.

How were the upright stones raised into position?

How were the great lintels placed across them?

Scholars have given a great deal of thought to these problems. They have borne in mind that the primitive builders had only the crudest tools and little knowledge of engineering.

This is how they think that the uprights were raised. First a hole about eight feet deep was dug. Three sides of this hole were straight up and down. The fourth was slanted. The side of the hole opposite the sloping side was lined with wood.

An upright was dragged to the hole on rollers and placed so that the bottom end stuck out over the sloping side of the hole. The other end of the stone was lifted a little at a time, being held up by logs placed under it in a criss-cross pattern. Once a certain height was reached, the stone would slide down into the hole. The wood on the opposite side prevented the wall of the hole from caving in as the stone slid into position.

At this stage, a sort of collar would be placed around the stone near the top and, using ropes attached to this, men would pull the stone into an upright position.

To lift the lintels into position, a platform of wood was probably built around the upright. First the lintel would be raised one or two feet and a platform built under it. Then it would be raised one or two feet above the platform and the height of the platform increased. At each stage the raising of the lintel would be done by teams of men using long logs of wood as levers.

At the top of each upright is a sticking up piece approaching nine inches high. These sticking up pieces are called tenons, and they slot into holes in the lintels to make them secure in position.

In 1953, a new discovery was made. Carved signs were found on some of the largest stones. Most of them were the shapes of bronze axe-heads in their actual

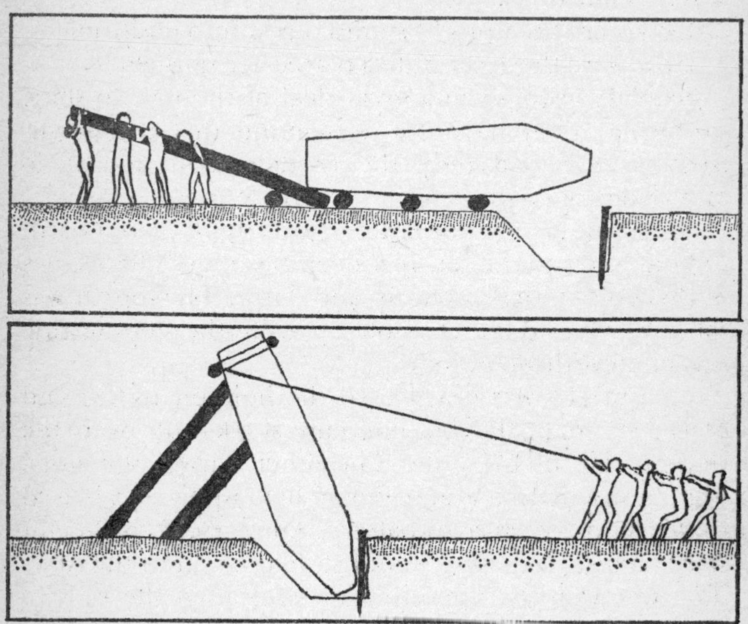

size. They were the kind of axes used in around 1600 B.C. There was also one carving of a dagger and this appeared to be of a kind used in Greece at that time.

The carvings were of no help in solving the mystery of Stonehenge. Indeed, they added a new element to the mystery. In tombs near Stonehenge beads and ornaments from Greece and other Mediterranean lands have been found. So some form of trade existed between these countries and Britain.

The idea has been put forward that someone from

Greece helped to design Stonehenge 3. One leading British archaeologist said, 'There is nothing else in all of Britain anything like Stonehenge. Whoever planned it had probably seen properly-designed buildings in Greece.'

However much archaeologists and other scholars have been able to discover about the building of Stonehenge, the final question defies them: Why was Stonehenge built?

Most experts agree that Stonehenge was a temple of some kind but they cannot suggest what kind of ceremonies took place inside it. The entrance to Stonehenge looks down the middle of the avenue towards sunrise on Midsummer Day (about 21st June). Because of this some people have suggested that Stonehenge was a place where the Sun was worshipped.

One of the massive stones at Stonehenge lies flat on the ground and this has come to be called the Altar Stone. This stone probably used to stand upright. But because of its position it gave rise to stories that Stonehenge was a place where sacrifices were once held— possibly sacrifices of human beings. There is no evidence to support this idea at all.

Astronomers studying the position of the circle of stones wondered whether they were somehow linked with positions of the Sun and also of the Moon. One idea was that the circle could be used somehow to foretell when an eclipse of the Sun or the Moon was going to take place.

The Sun and the Moon were both important to the prehistoric people who built Stonehenge. They depended upon the Sun for their crops and warmth while the Moon gave them light at night. To such people an eclipse of the Sun or the Moon might be an awful and frightening thing—perhaps a sign that the gods were displeased. Yet once an eclipse could be predicted, attitudes would change. Eclipses happening in a recognisable pattern might be looked upon as part of the normal behaviour of the gods.

Studies of the relationship of the position of the stones in Stonehenge with the positions of the Sun and Moon at various times proved nothing for a long time. Then, in 1961, Professor Hawkins fed information about the stones into a computer along with information about the positions of the Sun and Moon. He wanted to know if the positions of the stones were linked with positions of the Sun or Moon and the computer's answer appeared to be, 'Yes.' But it was not conclusive. So Professor Hawkins fed into the computer details of the positions of the Sun and the Moon not as they are today but as they were in 1500 B.C. He then found ten links with positions of the Sun and fourteen with positions of the Moon. For example, if a person stood at the centre of Stonehenge on 8th November or 5th February and looked over a certain stone, he would see the sunrise. If, from the same position, he looked over another stone on 6th May and 8th August, he would see the sunset. These are significant dates. Each is about forty-six days before or after Midwinter Day (21st December) or Midsummer Day (about 21st June).

Yet this still did not solve the mystery of Stonehenge. It is not clear what value links of this kind would have for the builders of Stonehenge. It has been suggested that Stonehenge was used as a kind of calendar. The position of the Sun on any day could be seen and related to known dates such as Midsummer Day. Perhaps Stonehenge helped Stone Age men to know when spring would be coming after the cruel winter. To them, such information would be very important.

No one knows the answer to the final mystery. Experts on Stonehenge do not agree among themselves about some things. Professor Hawkins's work with the computer is not accepted by many of them. A com-

puter's answer, they say, is only as good as the information fed into it, and some of the information fed
into his computer by Professor Hawkins was doubtful.

Perhaps we shall never know the answer to this
mystery. But one thing is certain. From the effort involved in building Stonehenge, the monument had a
great significance to the men who built it.

THE RIDDLE OF AIRLINER G–AGBB

Leslie Howard was one of the most famous film stars in the world. An Englishman, he was working and living in Hollywood, U.S.A., the centre of the world cinema industry in 1939. Then World War Two began. At once Howard returned to England. He said that he had come home to help in the war. 'I will do anything that I am wanted to do,' he stated.

In World War Two, there were many important jobs to do besides fighting with the Armed Forces. Films were being made for two reasons—to keep up people's spirits in Britain and also to show people in countries not taking part in the war how people in Britain felt about things. At some stage in the war, these countries might join in. The British wanted to provide good reasons for joining in on the British side.

Back in England, Leslie Howard began making films to help the war effort. The first was *Pimpernel Smith*. In this Howard played the part of a mild-seeming professor of archaeology rescuing Jews from Nazi Germany. The film called attention to the Germans' cruelty to the Jews. It also showed the bravery and cleverness of the English professor in spite of his easy-going ways. It was a splendid film for keeping up the spirits of people in Britain and also for showing to countries not taking part in the war.

In 1943, the British Council wanted to arrange for more British films to be shown in Spain and Portugal, two countries not taking part in the war. They had the idea of sending Leslie Howard out there. For one month he travelled from place to place giving lectures about the cinema and the theatre in Britain and showing films about the country. Everywhere he went his talks were a success. Howard was a quiet-mannered, fair-haired man, slight in build, and the Spanish and Portuguese liked him immensely. By the end of his tour, more than nine hundred cinemas in Spain and Portugal had agreed to show British films and, in Portugal, *Pimpernel Smith* was later voted the finest film of the year.

Howard was planning to fly back to England on 29th May but the British Council asked him to stay on in Portugal for a few more days. Howard's latest film, *The First of the Few*, was about to be shown for the first time there, and the British Council wanted him to be present.

The First of the Few was another ideal war-time film. In it Howard played the part of R. J. Mitchell, the designer of the Supermarine Spitfire. This was the fighter plane which helped the Royal Air Force to win the Battle of Britain and the title of the film came from some words of Winston Churchill about the British pilots in that battle—'Never in the field of human conflict have so many owed so much to so few.'

Howard readily agreed to stay on, and enjoyed his extra days in a hotel beside the sea at Estoril. At the time he wrote to a friend, 'Sitting by the side of the Atlantic Ocean, for the first time I am able to collect my thoughts.' He had had a busy time since returning to England from the United States. A third film, *The Lamp Still Burns,* was waiting to be completed when he got back from his latest trip.

Howard also wrote to the Director of the British Institute in Madrid. He had been hoping to talk to a group of children there but had too much to do to keep the engagement. He wrote to tell the Director how sorry he was about this, and asked whether he could send the children something from England to make up for their disappointment. This was the kind of thoughtful and considerate action Leslie Howard was noted for.

On the day of the first showing of *The First of the Few*, Howard was to have lunch with his friend and business manager, Alfred Chenhalls, and another man,

Neville Kearney of the British Council. They went into the bar for a drink before lunch and Kearney noticed an attractive woman among the people there. He knew her and thought that she was a German spy. To be sure, he went out and telephoned to the British Embassy in Lisbon. The woman was known there. She was a spy.

Neville Kearney returned to the bar. He was just in time to hear Howard saying, 'We're going home by the morning plane from Lisbon Airport on 1st June.' The woman spy was sitting near enough to have overheard these words.

Kearney was upset about this, and he warned Howard and Chenhalls to be careful what they said in public. Yet the movements of the two men could hardly have been kept a secret. Indeed, it came to light later that German agents had been following them around for some time. The Germans believed that anyone working for the British Council might be acting in some way as a British secret agent, and Leslie Howard was no exception.

Early on the morning of 1st June, Howard and Chenhalls were driven to Lisbon Airport in a car from the British Embassy. They were flying in a Douglas D.C.3. of K.L.M., the Royal Dutch Airline. Holland had been overrun by the Germans in 1940 but several crews of the airline had escaped. Now three of them were running a regular service between Lisbon and 'an airfield in Britain'. The destination was not generally revealed. It was, in fact, a civil airfield at Whitchurch, near Bristol.

Fourteen passengers were to travel in the D.C.3 which bore the code-letters G–AGBB. Apart from Howard and Chenhalls, most of them were diplomats or businessmen. At the last moment the number aboard was reduced to thirteen. The Reverend Arthur S. Holmes, vice-president of the English College in Lisbon, went aboard with the other passengers. An official was bringing him a parcel from the Customs—some gifts he was taking home. The man also brought a message. He said, 'You are wanted urgently at the English College.'

Rev. Holmes was puzzled. 'Did they say what for?' he asked.

'No. Just that you are wanted immediately.'

The clergyman collected his luggage and left the plane, and soon afterwards the D.C.3 took off. The time was half-past nine.

The airliner winged along the coast of Portugal and Spain to Cape Finisterre and then out across the Bay of Biscay. It never reached England. A message was received, 'I am being attacked by enemy aircraft.' After that, silence. . . .

Allied aircraft made a search in the area where the airliner had been attacked. Nothing was found—no survivors, no wreckage. Afterwards it was accepted that G–AGBB had been destroyed by enemy action.

The newspapers in England treated the news as a sensation.

AIRLINER SHOT DOWN: LESLIE HOWARD MISSING.

The film star was a tremendously popular figure. His loss was deeply felt. In addition, the idea of German aircraft attacking an unarmed civil airliner on a peaceful flight shocked people.

The Germans defended their action. They said that the airliner 'had camouflage paint, and was in no way distinguishable from a war plane.' This was untrue. The airliner bore the insignia of K.L.M.

Referring to the scene of the attack, the Germans said that the Bay of Biscay was 'a zone of operations where British aircraft are waging war against U–boats on their way to and from German bases.' They claimed that D.C.3s like the airliner had been used on bombing operations. Again, this was not true. The military version of the D.C.3, the Douglas C–47 or Dakota, was only used as a transport aircraft.

In time, the last flight of Douglas D.C.3 G–AGBB was reconstructed. Under her pilot, Captain Quirinas Tepas, she flew northwards towards the Bay of Biscay in a drizzle of fine rain. Every half hour the wireless operator, Cornelius Van Brugge, tapped out a signal to Lisbon Airport. It gave the estimated position of the plane.

After two hours of flying, the airliner was over Corunna and beginning the crossing of the Bay of Biscay. From this time onward, no more messages would be sent, except in an emergency. German aircraft operated over the Bay and it was better to keep radio silence.

Out over the Bay, visibility became clear. A single Junkers Ju88 twin-engined fighter-bomber was probably first seen from the D.C.3. At once Van Brugge tapped out a wireless signal which meant, 'I am being followed by an unidentified aircraft.' This was quickly followed by G–AGBB's last message: 'I am being attacked by enemy aircraft.'

Eight Ju88s had taken off from an airfield near Bordeaux in France half an hour after G–AGBB left Lisbon. Was this a routine flight? Were the aircraft providing cover for two U-boats crossing the Bay of Biscay? Or were they sent out as a result of a telephone call from Lisbon Airport? G–AGBB had taken off in full view of Germans in the offices of Deutsche Lufthansa, the German airline. Any one of them could have put through a telephone call.

Soon after that last message was sent, the eight Ju88s must have swept in, swathing the airliner with machine-gun and canon-fire. After the war, German records of the attack were found. They stated that the D.C.3 went down in flames and, as it did so, German pilots saw four figure in parachutes leap out of the door in the fuselage. Only two of the parachutes opened properly. Of these, one was on fire. No trace of any of the parachutes could be seen in the sea after the airliner had crashed.

There is a mystery about this story of four parachutists. It was not usual for passengers on the flight to be issued with parachutes. Could any of the thirteen passengers aboard the airliner have been issued with them? Were there four people aboard considered to be so important that they were given special treatment? Or were the German pilots mistaken? Perhaps four people simply fell from the blazing aircraft as it crashed into

the sea. Certainly no one at Lisbon Airport saw parachutes go aboard the airliner as it prepared to take off,
and they were bulky objects to conceal.

Why was G–AGBB shot down? Attempts to solve
this mystery have centred upon Leslie Howard. Of the
thirteen passengers on board, he was the best known.
Neville Kearney believed that he was the passenger the
Germans wanted to kill. He suggested that Josef Goebbels, the Nazi leader in charge of propaganda, gave
the order for Howard's death. Goebbels would be only
too well aware of the value of Howard's films to the
British war effort both inside Britain and outside it.

On the face of it, this appears a far-fetched notion.
But supposing that, in addition, Howard was suspected
of acting as a British secret agent on his travels in Spain
and Portugal. The fact that he was followed by German
spies indicates a great deal of interest in his activities.

The circumstances under which Howard went on
the airliner have been closely inspected. It turned out
that, shortly before the flight, Reverend Holmes had
received a telephone call from Lisbon Airport. It was
about room on the plane. He was told: 'Mr. Leslie
Howard is travelling with a party of four, and we can
only find seats for three of them. If it should be neces-
sary, I wonder whether, as a favour to Mr. Howard,
you would mind if we put you on a later plane.'

Rev. Holmes had readily agreed. 'Do you still want
me to come to the airport?' he asked.

He was told, Yes. Efforts were being made to fit every-
body in. As things turned out, of course, Rev. Holmes
was given a seat on the airliner but did not take it.

It is not known who made up Howard's 'party of
four'. One member would be Alfred Chenhalls. Who
were the other two? They received special treatment
in the way of being provided with seats. Were they important enough to attract the attention of the Germans?
Were they important enough to have been issued with

parachutes?

There were three possibilities for Howard's other two companions. They were: Gordon Maclean, Inspector of Consulates for the British Foreign Office who had been visiting Madrid and Lisbon; Berthold Israel who had been sent out to Lisbon by the Colonial Office in connection with the Jewish Agency in Palestine; and Tyrell Shervington, a businessman with Shell-Mex in Portugal said to be suspected by the Germans of being a spy. Howard and Chenhalls had often met Maclean and Israel at the British Embassy in Lisbon. Was it likely that *Luftwaffe* aircraft should be sent out on a special mission in order to kill one of these three men?

Is it possible that the Germans thought that some other person of importance was in the airliner? At this time, the Prime Minister of Britain, Winston Churchill, was in Algiers (North Africa) making plans with other war leaders for the future conduct of the war in Europe. Alfred Chenhalls was, like Churchill, a man of heavy build. Like Churchill, he often smoked cigars. It has been suggested that Chenhalls was mistaken for Churchill and that the airliner was shot down in the hope of killing him.

In his memoirs of World War Two, Churchill referred to this idea. He wrote: 'As my presence in North Africa had been fully reported, the Germans were exceptionally vigilant, and this led to a tragedy which distressed me. The regular commercial aircraft was about to start from the Lisbon airfield when a thickset man smoking a cigar walked up and was thought to be a passenger on it. The German agents therefore signalled that I was on board. Although these passenger planes had plied unmolested for many months between Portugal and England, a German war plane was instantly ordered out, and the defenceless aircraft was ruthlessly shot down.'

Churchill appears, in this passage, to believe that the

Germans made a tragic error. Yet he went on: 'It is difficult to understand how anyone could imagine that with all the resources of Great Britain at my disposal I should have flown home in broad daylight. We, of course, made a wide loop out by night from Gibraltar into the ocean and arrived home without incident.'

It *is* difficult to believe that the Germans mistook

Chenhalls for Churchill, particularly since their agents had been shadowing him and Howard for some time.

Churchill was wrong in stating that there had been no previous attacks on aircraft flying the Portugal–England route. In November 1942 G-AGBB was attacked 250 miles from England on the run from Lisbon and, six weeks before G-AGBB was shot down, on 19th April, 1943, six Ju88s had opened fire on another K.L.M. D.C.3 on its way to Whitchurch.

According to some accounts, only the superb flying skill of the pilot of the second aircraft had saved it from being shot down. But for an unarmed D.C.3 to escape from six Ju88s *intent on shooting it down* would not only take superb flying skill—it would take a miracle. The question arises: Were the Ju88s simply harassing the airliners on both occasions? The pointless shooting down of an unarmed civil airliner flying from a neutral country would not have helped Germany in the propaganda war. Recall how they strove to justify their action after shooting down G-AGBB.

After the attack in April, it was considered whether to make the flights between Lisbon and Whitchurch at night in the future. There were difficulties about this, and it was decided, for the time being, to carry on with the daylight flights. The tragedy of 1st June was the result of this decision.

It is entirely possible that the Germans had decided to put a stop to the Lisbon–Whitchurch flights. Twice they had shown that they could intercept them. These warnings had gone unheeded. So an airliner had to be shot down, and it happened to be G-AGBB. The fact that Leslie Howard was on board was a tragic coincidence.

At the end of the war, the records of KG 40 Bomber Group of the *Luftwaffe* were inspected. The fighter wing that sent out the eight Ju88s was attached to this group. The details of their flight on 1st June, 1943, were located but no secret instructions came to light. If someone on board G-AGBB was the target of the operation, this fact was not included in the details of it.

So the mystery remains. Why was the Douglas D.C.3 G-AGBB shot down? Was Leslie Howard the target of the Ju88s operation? Could the Germans have believed that Winston Churchill was on board? Was the target someone else in Howard's 'party of four'?

One curious incident makes the mystery more intriguing. The Reverend Arthur S. Holmes, you will recall, was asked to leave the airliner at the last moment before take-off. He went back to the English College at once. There he could find no one who knew anything about the telephone call which caused him to return.

Who made that telephone call? Was it someone who knew that G-AGBB was doomed and did not want Rev. Holmes to die?

After all these years, it is unlikely that this question will ever be answered.

WHO KILLED THE PRINCES IN THE TOWER?

ONE DAY IN July 1674, some workmen pulling down a flight of stone stairs in the Tower of London made a startling discovery. Under one of the steps they found a wooden chest containing two small skeletons. In those days, news did not travel fast, but travel it did. Wherever news of the find was heard, heads wagged sagely. 'There's no doubt about it,' someone would say. 'It's the poor, little Princes in the Tower, turned up after all these years.'

King Charles II had the bones inspected by his own doctor. The doctor said that they belonged to two boys aged about eight and thirteen. Charles asked the great architect, Sir Christopher Wren, to design a marble urn to hold the bones. In time this task was completed and, in 1678, the urn, with the bones inside, was placed in Westminster Abbey, the final resting place of royalty in England.

But this did not put an end to the mystery of the Princes in the Tower. It may have answered one of the questions: What had become of their bodies? But it did not answer the biggest question of all: Who killed them?

The Princes in the Tower were Edward and Richard, sons of King Edward IV. They lived at a time when there were constant quarrels over the throne of England —in the days of the Wars of the Roses.

The Wars of the Roses were fought between supporters of two families and they received their name from the badges the families wore. Followers of the Duke of York wore a white rose; supporters of the rival house of Lancaster wore a red rose. Both families were descended from sons of King Edward III.

In 1455, Henry VI of the House of Lancaster was King of England. Richard, Duke of York, raised an army against him and they fought a battle at St. Albans, Hertfordshire. The King's forces were defeated and Henry was taken prisoner.

Henry became seriously ill and the Council of State made Richard Protector of England. But when Henry was better, the post was taken from Richard.

More battles followed. Henry was defeated at Northampton in 1460 and again taken prisoner. But his wife, Queen Margaret, had escaped to Scotland with their son, and she marched into England with an army. Yorkists and Lancastrians met once more in the Battle of Wakefield (1460) and the Lancastrians won. Richard was killed and his head, decorated with a paper crown, was hung on the walls of the city of York.

Queen Margaret and her army marched on. They beat the Yorkists in the Second Battle of St. Albans (1461) and were joined by Henry VI. But afterwards they were routed at Towton, Yorkshire, by an army led by Edward Plantagenet, Duke of York and son of Richard. He had vowed to avenge his father's death.

Edward Plantagenet was eighteen years old, a handsome young man six feet tall and slimly built. The Council of State gave him the crown of England and, as Edward IV, he reigned successfully for a time with the help of a wily statesman named Richard Neville, Earl of Warwick.

Yet Edward IV's throne was not secure. In 1464 a rising by the Lancastrians was defeated at Hexham (Northumberland). Afterwards the old king, Henry VI, was made prisoner and locked in the Tower of London. Later the Earl of Warwick turned traitor to Edward IV. He set free Henry VI and restored him to the throne. Experts in history give the scheming Warwick the nickname of 'the King-maker'.

Edward IV fled to Holland and returned with a strong army. He defeated forces led by the traitorous Earl of Warwick at Barnet, Hertfordshire, on Easter Sunday 1471 and Warwick was killed. Later Queen Margaret was defeated at Tewkesbury in Gloucestershire. Her son, Prince Edward, was murdered and Henry VI was put to death in the Tower of London.

Yorkists had gained the upper hand and there were no more battles of the Roses in Edward IV's reign. He is said to have ruled well although he was not an active person. He loved eating and drinking and became grossly fat and, on 9th April, 1483, died suddenly at the age of forty-two.

Edward left two sons, Edward, aged twelve and a half years, and Richard, aged ten. The elder became King Edward V but, in his will, Edward IV asked his brother, Richard, Duke of Gloucester, to govern England until the boy was old enough to rule himself.

At the time of his father's death, Prince Edward was staying at Ludlow Castle in Shropshire with his uncle, Lord Rivers. Rivers was the brother of the queen, Elizabeth, and she did not want the Duke of Gloucester to have control over her son. She wanted Edward to be crowned at once and to rule through the Council of State.

On 24th April, Lord Rivers and Edward left Ludlow for London with a large party of men. By this time, the Duke of Gloucester knew their plans. He had been staying at Middleham Castle his home in Yorkshire. Now he left for London with a smaller force.

The two parties met at Stony Stratford (Buckinghamshire). The Duke had Rivers arrested. He told

Edward that his uncle had been plotting against him and had him sent to Yorkshire as a prisoner. Rivers was executed without trial outside Pontefract Castle one month later.

Meantime, to be safe from Richard, Queen Elizabeth had fled with the rest of her family from the Palace of Westminster. She went into Westminster Abbey. No one would dare to harm her or her children in such a holy place.

Richard travelled on to London with Edward V. He did not immediately make plans for the boy's coronation. Instead, he lodged the boy in the royal apartments in the Tower of London.

The Council of State agreed that Richard should be Protector of England and look after Edward V. A new date was fixed for the coronation—22nd June. Later this was postponed again to 2nd November, and Queen Elizabeth agreed to let Edward V's younger brother, Prince Richard, go to stay with him in the Tower.

It seems that, at this point, the Duke of Gloucester had begun to think about being king himself. One of his supporters criticised him openly and at once Richard told the Council of State that the man was a traitor to England. He was promptly put to death.

Then a startling story came to light. The Bishop of Bath and Wells said that King Edward IV had agreed to marry Lady Elizabeth Butler before he married Queen Elizabeth. In the eyes of the Church and the law of the land, Edward and Queen Elizabeth had not been legally married. Therefore, Edward was not a legitimate son and had no claim to the throne of England.

Some experts in history say that this story was not true. The fact remains that the Council of State said that Richard, Duke of Gloucester should be the king, and he came to the throne on 26th June, 1483. Twelve-year-old Edward V had been King of England for just seventy-eight days.

Richard III was known as Crookback for he had a hump on his back. He also had a withered arm and, according to some writers, features like the Devil. William Shakespeare wrote a play about him, and in the play the King is a villain of the worst kind. Yet portraits painted during his lifetime show that Richard was handsome. They show a kindly face with thoughtful eyes and a firm chin.

Richard was a brave soldier. At the age of sixteen he fought in the battles of Barnet and Tewkesbury and led his men well. He read a great deal and he ruled wisely. During his reign, hundreds of useful Acts of Parliament were passed. He was particularly well liked in his home county of Yorkshire.

Yet Richard acted ruthlessly against his enemies. This much is clear from the way he got rid of Lord Rivers and others.

On 6th July, 1483, Richard III was crowned. He still had the two princes, Edward and Richard, lodged in the royal apartments in the Tower of London. They had sometimes been seen playing in the garden or peering out of the windows.

How often were the princes seen after Richard's coronation? Not often, say most accounts.

In October 1483 rumours began to spread. It was said that Richard had had the two boys murdered. Yet it is not clear why he should have done this. Edward was no longer a rival for the throne.

In January 1484, the Chancellor of France accused the English King of murdering the princes. He had an obvious reason for this. At this time, a Lancastrian, Henry Tudor, was in France plotting against Richard III. It would suit Henry's purpose to have Richard III's name blackened.

In August 1485, Henry Tudor landed with an army in Wales and marched into the Midlands of England. On 22nd August, on a large, sloping field outside Bosworth (Leicestershire), the last battle of the Wars of the Roses took place.

Richard III, with his crown over his helmet, led his forces against the invaders. It was a hard-fought battle. At its height Richard called for reserves of men to join in. They had been standing at the side of the field under

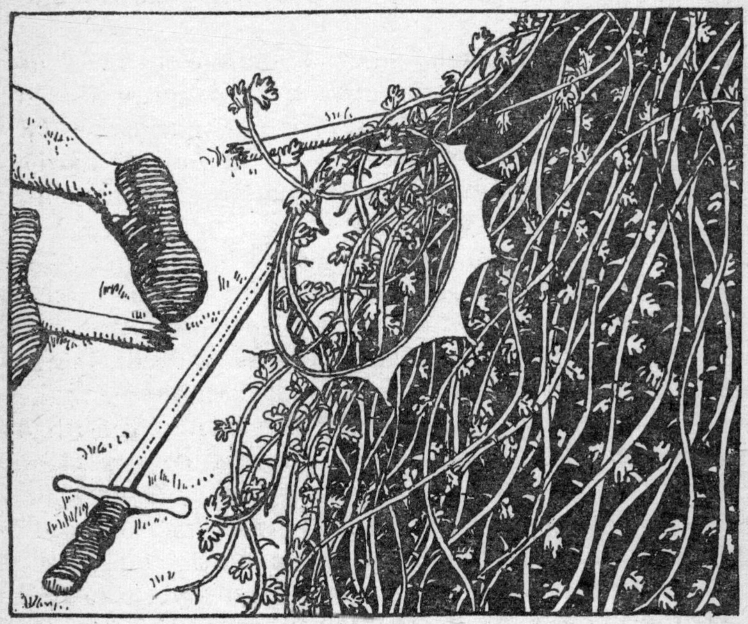

the command of Lord William Stanley. To Richard's dismay, the reserves swept in and attacked his forces. Stanley had changed sides.

Crying 'Traitor! Traitor!' and slashing left and right with a great battle-axe, Richard charged towards Henry Tudor's bodyguard. He killed Henry's standard-bearer before a blow from behind brought him off his horse.

Men bent over, stabbing and cutting, and Richard III died a warrior's death. His crown had fallen from his helmet and was caught in a hawthorn bush. Lord Stanley picked it up and presented it to Henry Tudor.

Amid cheers from all sides, Henry VII put the crown on his head.

From the start of his reign, Henry VII set out to be liked. To show that the Wars of the Roses were over, he married Edward V's sister, Elizabeth of York, and he invented a new badge for himself. It was a combination of the white rose and the red rose and he called it the Tudor Rose.

He also, so it is said, set out to blacken the name of Richard III systematically. An Italian writer, Polydore Virgil, was paid to write a history of the times and he included in it every claim made against Richard's character. So did other writers of history in the times of the Tudor kings and queens, including Sir Thomas More.

In *The History of Richard III*, Sir Thomas More wrote a detailed account of how Richard was supposed to have had the two young princes put to death. It was soon after his coronation. Richard had set out on a tour of the kingdom, and he sent a servant, John Green, with a message to Sir Robert Brackenbury, the Contable of the Tower of London. The message told Brackenbury to kill the princes.

Brackenbury refused. So Richard sent Sir James Tyrell to see him. Tyrell had orders to collect the keys of the Tower from Brackenbury. The Constable handed them over and Tyrell used them. He sent his groom, John Dighton, and a jailer named Miles Forest into the royal apartments and there they smothered the sleeping children. Afterwards, Tyrell had the two men bury the bodies under the stairs in the White Tower.

Tyrell led a checkered career. In 1502 he was in command of a fortress near Calais in France, and he surrendered it to the Yorkist Earl of Suffolk, a nephew of Richard III. On his return to England, Tyrell was tried for treason and condemned to death. Before he was executed, he was said to have confessed to his part in the death of the Princes in the Tower.

William Shakespeare lived in Tudor times and he told the same story as Thomas More in his play, *Richard III*.

But about the same time a different version of the crime was published in Burgundy. According to this,

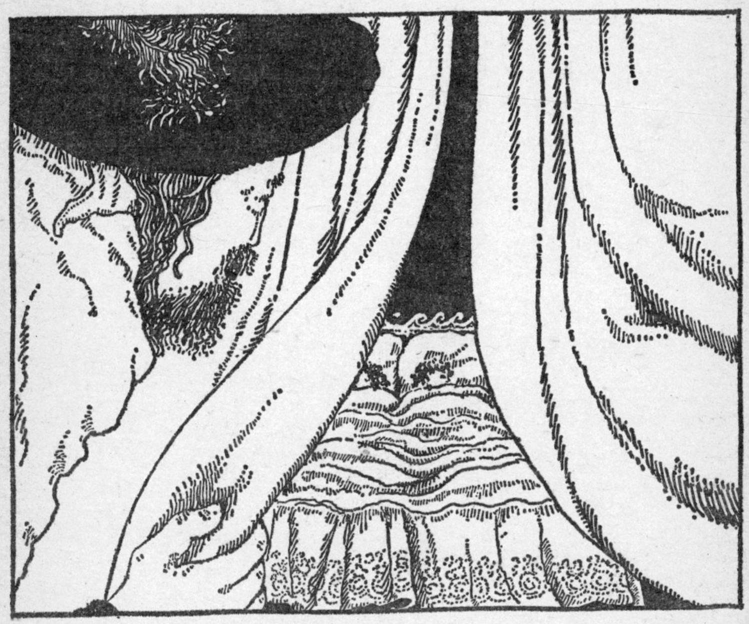

the princes were walled up in a room in the Tower and then left to suffocate or starve to death.

Today experts in history are not so ready to accept either that King Richard III was a wicked king or that he had the princes murdered. There is, first of all, the question of why he should do so. He stood to gain nothing from the death of the princes. He was already secure as King of England.

There is also the attitude of the princes' family. In March 1484 the old Queen Elizabeth finally left Westminster Abbey and Richard gave her a pension of 700 marks a year. Her daughter, Elizabeth of York, and her sisters attended the Court of King Richard and danced there at Christmas 1484. Is the behaviour of Queen Elizabeth and her daughters likely if they knew—or even suspected—that Richard had murdered the princes?

What are the alternatives?

Perhaps the princes were taken out of England. From the start of the affair, rumours said that this had happened. Sir George Buck, writing later than Tudor times in about 1640, said: 'The young princes were embarked in a ship at Tower Wharf and set safe on shore beyond the seas.' Buck was a descendant of Sir John Buck, an official of King Richard's household.

But, if the princes escaped, what became of them?

In 1490, a young man now known as Perkin Warbeck appeared at the court of the Duchess of Burgundy, a sister of King Edward IV, and claimed to be Richard, Duke of York, the younger of the Princes in the Tower.

Warbeck laid claim to the throne of England and travelled to Ireland to rouse support. He was helped by King James IV of Scotland, later, and he landed in Cornwall with an army in 1498.

Warbeck's rising met with no success. His troops were soon routed and he was arrested and sent to the Tower of London. There he wrote a confession. He admitted that he was not Richard, Duke of York, and had, in fact, been born in Flanders. After trying to escape, he was executed in 1499.

Warbeck's adventure is believed by some people to have caused the production of Sir James Tyrell's confession three years later. If the Princes in the Tower were known to be dead, there could be no more danger from people pretending to be them.

Buck believed that Perkin Warbeck really was Richard, Duke of York. As to his brother, Edward, he believed that, after his escape, he died of illness.

It is asked why Warbeck pretended to be Richard

and not Edward. Possibly he looked more like the younger prince. Perhaps, say some people, it was well known that Edward was dead. But, in this case, what of Richard? Where was he while Warbeck was taking his place? *Was Warbeck, in fact, Richard, the younger of the Princes in the Tower?*

There is one other possible explanation of what happened to the Princes in the Tower. It was never voiced or written down in Tudor times but it is today. Namely, that the two princes were murdered by Henry VII.

Henry had more reason to murder the princes than Richard III had. He was planning to marry their sister, Elizabeth of York. In order to do this, he had to have her known to be a legitimate daughter of Edward IV and an Act of Parliament was prepared to show this. But if Elizabeth was a legitimate daughter, then Edward was a legitimate son. Therefore, he had more right to the throne than Henry Tudor. He might, once again, become Edward V.

If the two princes were murdered in the Tower of London, they were murdered by order of either Richard III or Henry VII. One fact would show which was guilty: the date the princes died. This fact is not known.

Could the princes have still been alive on 22nd August, 1485, the date of the Battle of Bosworth Field? If they were still alive at Christmas 1484 (when Princess Elizabeth of York, their sister, danced at Richard III's Court) they might well have been. In this case, in order to make his throne secure, Henry VII might have wasted no time in having them put to death.

The next rightful heir to the throne after the princes was Edward Plantagenet, Earl of Warwick. Henry VII had him imprisoned in the Tower and later executed.

No one can be sure that the bones in the urn in Westminster Abbey belonged to the Princes in the Tower. Yet it does seem probable that they did.

In 1933, the bones were examined by a modern expert. He was William Wright, a professor at London Hospital Medical College and President of the Anatomical Society. Strangely enough, animal bones were found among them. But most of the bones belonged to two children, either boys or girls, and these children were roughly of the ages of the two princes.

The Professor was unable to say when the children had died. The bones were laid out with the skulls and the probable heights of the children were worked out. They were 4 ft. $9\frac{1}{2}$ in. and 4 ft. $6\frac{1}{2}$ in. These were, respectively, equal to the average heights of modern children aged fourteen and twelve.

Most people in the Middle Ages were smaller than people of today. But King Edward IV was taller than most men of his time. Probably his sons would be taller, too.

Perhaps Prince Edward, at fourteen, was the same height as a modern boy of fourteen. He probably would not have been that height at an earlier age. At the date of the Battle of Bosworth Field, Prince Edward would have been fourteen years nine months old. This makes Edward's murder by King Henry VII seem possible. The same is true of Prince Richard. He would have been twelve in 1485.

How did the princes die? Most accounts have suggested that they were smothered in their sleep. Professor Wright found a stain on one of the skulls. Such stains occurred in death by smothering. But, on the other hand, the stain might have been caused by a rusty nail.

So the mystery of the Princes in the Tower, once thought to have been solved, remains. In England today, the Bosworth Society believe that Richard III had the boys murdered. But the Richard III Society believe that Henry VII was the guilty man. On the evidence available, neither can be sure.

THE LOCH NESS MONSTER

In 1933, a new road was opened along the northern shore of Loch Ness, in Scotland, running from Fort Augustus to Inverness. Early in the morning of 22nd May of that year, Mr. John McKay and his wife travelled by car along this road and returned with a startling story. They had, they said, seen a large beast crossing the road ahead of them. As they approached, it plunged into the waters of the Loch.

This became the first widely-known account in modern times of a sighting of the Loch Ness Monster. The McKays described the beast they had seen. It had a great, barrel-like body and a neck about ten feet long. It looked like a dinosaur of prehistoric times.

The story of the Loch Ness Monster was reported in the newspapers and it created a sensation. Before the year ended, one hundred and fifty-four other people claimed to have seen something of the Monster.

Opinion was divided on the subject. One group of people seriously believed that there might be a creature unknown to science living in the Loch. Another group believed that all the stories were false or the result of people's imagination. Later Sir Arthur Keith, a leading anthropologist was to say, 'It's not a problem for zoologists but for psychologists'; in other words, people who thought that they saw the monster were imagining things.

It was pointed out more than once that having a

Loch Ness Monster was good for the people who sold things to visitors to the area. 'It's a stunt,' said the doubters. 'People running hotels and cafes up there have organised it. They must be doing a roaring trade these days.'

Comedians on the music-hall stage and on the radio found that they could get easy laughs by telling jokes

about the Monster. Then footprints of a large creature were found in the mud on the shores of the Loch. Plaster casts were made of them and sent to the British Museum.

The result was hilarious. The prints had been made by the foot of a female hippopotamus. Someone had borrowed part of a stuffed animal and made the footprints for fun!

But meantime, people taking the Loch Ness Monster seriously had called attention to an interesting fact. The idea of monsters in the lochs of Scotland was not new.

From time to time in the past, stories had been told about them.

The oldest account of what appears to be the Loch Ness Monster is to be found in the life of St. Columba written by St. Adamnan in 679–704. Columba was abbot of the monastery on the Isle of Iona in the sixth century and travelled widely in the Highlands preaching the word of God. This is Adamnan's account of Columba's encounter with the Monster in the River Ness which flows out of the Loch to the Moray Firth.

'When the Saint was in the province of the Picts, he had to cross the River Ness. On reaching the bank, he saw villagers burying a poor fellow who, they said, a little before had been swimming there. A water-beast with the most savage jaws had caught and bitten him. Some of them had put out in a boat but too late to do more than drag the river to recover the poor corpse.

'The Saint listened to this and said, "All the same, one of our company must swim to the opposite shore and steer the boat there back to me." When he heard this command of the worthy Saint, Luigni Mocu-min instantly obeyed, stripped to his shirt, and dived into the water.

'His former prey had sharpened the monster's appetite rather than assuaged it. He was lying hidden in deep water. But feeling the surface disturbed by the swimmer, up he came with a roar, jaws wide open, making straight for Luigni in midstream.

'The Saint saw it, and while the natives and even the brethren were terror-stricken, he just raised his holy hand to save him, drew the sign of the Cross in the empty air, and commanded the fierce beast in the name of God, saying, "No further! Do not touch him! Quick! Back you go!" The beast was so near Luigni that there was but a pole's length between. But at the Saint's call it drew back as quickly as if hauled by cables, and flew away.

'The brothers saw the beast go, saw their comrade Luigni back in the boat safe and sound, and with great wonder gave glory to God for the blessed man. And the heathen natives, seeing with their own eyes so great a miracle, were constrained to say, "Great is the god of the Christians!"'

One Duncan Campbell is said to have seen a similar monster in about 1527. 'This terrible beast—issuing out of the water early one morning in midsummer, he did very easily and without any force or straining of himself overthrow huge oaks with his tail and therewith killed outright three men that hunted him with three strokes of his tail, the rest of them saving themselves in trees thereabouts, while the aforesaid monster returned to the loch.'

The Chronicle of Fortingall, published in 1870, also includes a reference to a monster, but this is in another loch. 'There was a monstrous fish seen in Lochfyne, having great in the head thereof, and at times would stand above the water as high as the mast of a ship.'

Constance Whyte in a book about the Loch Ness Monster, *More than a Legend*, refers to a map of Loch Tay in the Bodleian Library at Oxford. It is dated 1325–50 and bears the notes, 'Waves without wind, fish without fin, and a floating island . . . The fish they speak of as having no fins are a kind of snake, and therefore no wonder!'

Vague stories of monsters in various Scottish lochs had been known among locals for many years before, in 1933, interest in the Loch Ness Monster became widespread.

Early in the morning of 22nd July that year, a Mr. and Mrs. Spicer put the Monster in the news once more. They returned from a drive with a remarkable story. They had, they said, seen 'a most extraordinary form of animal' crossing the road ahead of them and about twenty yards from Loch Ness. This creature had a neck about twelve feet long. It was a little thicker than an elephant's trunk, and it formed a number of arches. The animal's body was large and clumsy-looking. They could not see its legs owing to a dip in the road.

Mr. and Mrs. Spicer saw the creature from a distance of about two hundred yards. They estimated the overall length of it as twenty-five feet and the height of the body as four feet.

Mr. and Mrs. Spicer's story stimulated popular interest in the Monster, and Bertram Mills Circus offered £20,000 to anyone who could capture the creature for them.

Before the year was ended, a photograph of the Monster was produced. This was taken by Mr. Hugh Gray. Mr. Gray was walking along a footpath from the village of Foyers, about thirty feet above the shores of the Loch. Suddenly he saw the still waters become disturbed about one hundred yards from the shore. As he watched, he saw what appeared to be a large creature. It rose about a yard above the surface of the Loch and appeared to be about forty feet long.

Mr. Gray had a small box camera with him and he took several snapshots. He did this quickly for, in a couple of minutes, the object he had seen had disappeared.

Mr. Gray took his roll of film to a chemist's shop in Inverness. Unfortunately, only one of his photographs was clear enough to be worth printing. It showed a long, extended shape lying in the water. Later a man from Kodak Film inspected the negative of this photograph and said that it showed no sign of having been tampered with. In other words, Mr. Gray's photograph was not a fake.

On the other hand, what it showed was only an unknown object in the water. The object might have been one of many things; for example, a floating tree trunk.

Mr. Gray was vague about what he had seen. He said, 'I cannot give any definite opinion of size except that it was very great. It was a dark-greyish colour. The skin was glistening and appeared smooth.'

At one o'clock in the morning of 5th January, 1934, Arthur Grant was returning home from Inverness by motor-cycle close to Loch Ness and, he claimed, almost ran into the Monster. It was a moonlight night and he said that he saw a huge creature with a long neck. It lumbered across the road, crashed through some undergrowth and fell into the Loch with a loud splash. Leaping from his motor-cycle, Grant rushed to the water's edge but all he saw was a series of ripples.

Mr. Grant, who was studying to be a vet, was quite positive about what he had seen. He said, 'Knowing something of natural history, I can say that I have never seen anything in my life like the animal that I saw.' Mr. Grant described the creature he saw as being fifteen–twenty feet long with a long neck and a small head like that of an eel or snake. He estimated that the head was six feet above the ground. He said that the creature's body was round, with massive hindquarters and a tail, rounded at the end, five–six feet long. He thought that there were two sets of flippers.

Mr. Grant's story failed to convince people that there was a Loch Ness Monster. The doubters commented, 'There isn't a shred of proof. Mr. Grant could have been mistaken in what he saw. Shadows of trees in the moonlight could have tricked him. It has happened before.'

But three months later a new and better photograph was produced. It was taken by a surgeon from London using a telephoto lens, and it appeared to show the head and neck of the Monster rising out of the waters of the Loch.

The surgeon was motoring along the road beside Loch Ness early in the morning, driving towards Inverness. He noticed a disturbance in the water 200–300 yards from the near shore and at once stopped to take his photograph.

The photograph was published in the *Daily Mail* and caused a sensation. If this picture did not show the Loch Ness Monster, what did it show? There, in silhouette, appeared to be the long neck topped by a small

head—the Monster as it had been so often described. Below could be seen lines of wash indicating the movement of a large body through the water.

The surgeon's photograph was not clear enough to provide *proof* that there was a monster in Loch Ness. Arguments on the topic went on.

In June 1934, Alex Campbell, a water bailiff, reported seeing the Monster. Later he said, 'The early morning mist was clearing fast as I came out of my cottage on the banks of Loch Ness. As the mist shredded away under the warm sunlight, I witnessed the most incredible sight I have seen in my forty years as water bailiff on Scotland's biggest loch. Something rose from the water like a monster of prehistoric times, measuring a full thirty feet from tip to tail. It had a long, sinuous neck and a flat, reptilian head. Its skin was greyish black, tough-looking, and, just behind where the neck joined the body, was a giant hump like that on a camel, though many times bigger. I pinched myself hard, but it was no dream. The Loch Ness Monster out there in the water was real and tangible. For several minutes it lay there contentedly, basking in the early sunlight.

'The sound of a couple of herring drifters approaching broke the spell, and, as the drifters came nearer, it lowered its long neck and dived under the dark surface of the loch, disappearing in a turmoil of water and sending up a miniature tidal wave.'

Unlike others who had claimed to have seen the Monster, Mr. Campbell was a skilled observer. But his words cut no ice with the doubters. If they were to believe in the Loch Ness Monster, they wanted proof, not stories. In July 1934, Sir Edward Mountain set out to try to obtain proof.

Sir Edward took an expedition to the Loch. Twenty men watched the waters from nine o'clock in the morning until darkness with cameras always ready. The expedition spent thirty days at the Loch. Some still photographs were obtained and some 16 mm. film of something in the water. But they proved nothing. Some sightings were reported but, again, they were not conclusive. The expedition added little definite to people's knowledge of the Loch Ness Monster.

After Sir Edward Mountain's, no further expeditions were organised before the start of World War Two in 1939. Interest in the Monster died down. Occasionally there was news of a new sighting, generally in the summer. This is the period that the newspapers call the 'silly season', the period when, through holidays, there is usually a shortage of serious news.

During World War Two, the waters of Loch Ness were under the control of the Royal Navy. Visitors to the area were few and most people had little time to spare to think about the Monster. Yet, in May 1943, a member of the Royal Observer Corps, Mr. C. B. Farrel, reported seeing the Monster at a distance of 250 yards. Mr. Farrel was watching for enemy bombers and he had binoculars with him. He reported seeing through these a body twenty-five–thirty feet long and a 'graceful neck' sticking out of the water to a height of four–five feet. The eyes, he said, were large and prominent and on the back of the creature's neck was a curious projection like a fin.

With the end of the war in 1945, tourist traffic to Loch Ness began again and, with it, reports of sightings of the Monster. But these reports never created a sensation like the sightings of the thirties. They were curiosities, oddities. Perhaps people had grown more scientific-minded. Certainly the idea of an unknown creature living in Loch Ness was not one many people would consider without absolute proof.

In 1951, Mr. Lachlan Stewart, a woodsman working for the Forestry Commission, produced a new photograph. His story was that, one morning at half-past six, he had seen something large moving in the Loch. He called to a friend who was staying with him and, together, they hurried down to the shore. What they saw then, they said, was three separate triangular humps in the water with a small head on a long neck ahead of the first hump. Mr. Stewart took a photograph of the object with a small box camera. The photograph shows something in the water; but it did nothing to convince doubters.

Indeed, in 1956, in a booklet *Scientific Research* from the British Museum, the following passage was printed: 'The most famous case of the unsubmitted specimen is that of the "Loch Ness Monster", in which the ingenuity of suggestions as to the nature of the animal concerned has been equalled only by the powers of imagination of some observers. The only scientific evidence to which the Museum can point in explanation is the report, published in the *Glasgow Sunday Post* of 27th July, 1952, of some observations made with a theodolite by Mr. Andrew McAfee. At a distance of 300 yards, he saw the three dark humps which characterise the descriptions of the "Monster". With his theodolite, however, he was able to observe that the humps were shadows, and that they remained stationary while the ripples and wash of the water moved past them and gave the humps the appearance of movement. The phenomenon would therefore be one of waves and water-currents.'

With these words, Science dismissed the Loch Ness Monster; but the Monster refused to be dismissed. In 1959, Mr. Tim Dinsdale, an aviation engineer, began a careful study of the stories of the Monster. He collected one hundred separate accounts of sightings recorded over twenty-six years from May 1933 to September 1958 and he analysed them. This analysis brought out the following facts.

Sightings of the Monster have been reported throughout the whole period but mostly in 1933 and 1934. Perhaps, once the creature had become something of a joke, people grew cautious of reporting sightings for fear of being laughed at.

Eighty-five per cent of the sightings were made between dawn and 9.30 a.m. This might suggest that the Monster was a night creature. On the other hand, it had been reported seen right around the clock.

Reports about the head and neck suggest that the neck must be nine–ten feet long. The head is tiny in relation to the size of the creature's body and scarcely thicker than the neck, being flat on top. The eyes are

near the top of the head. Sometimes they are said to be
large, sometimes like slits. They do not appear to be
like the eyes of a fish.

In five per cent of the sightings, reference was made
to something sticking out on the neck, like a mane or

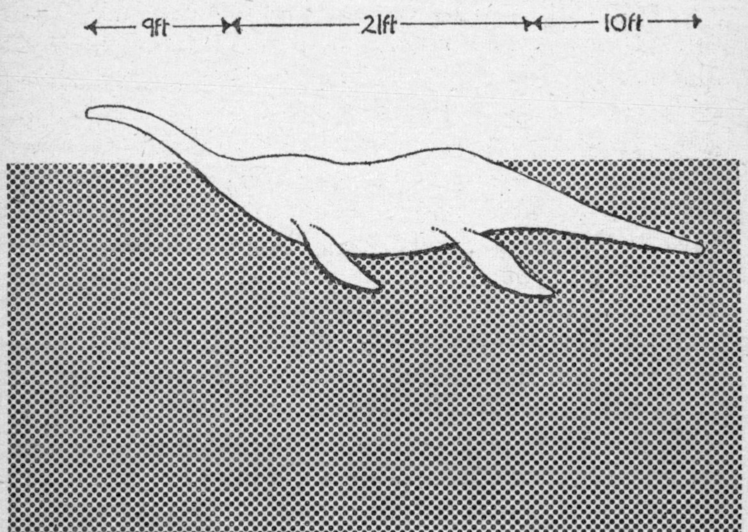

frill such as some reptiles have (and dinosaurs used to
have).

Most reports describe the body as being very large.
People who claim to have seen the creature in the water
often referred to humps. Some reports referred to a
single hump, some to as many as twelve. Sometimes the
humps were said to be triangular, sometimes rounded.

Only thirteen per cent of sightings include references
to limbs, fins or paddles. From these it appears that the
creature may use two pairs of fins or paddles to propel
it through the water.

Only eleven per cent of sightings referred to a tail.
This appears to be longer than six feet.

The overall length of the creature appears to be more than thirty feet.

Over one quarter of the sightings referred to colour and these indicate that the creature is grey like an elephant or reddish-brown.

Fifteen per cent of sightings described the creature as having skin of various textures; none referred to scales. Dinsdale concluded that the body might have a 'tough, warty hide' although the neck appeared to be smooth.

Mr. Dinsdale had built himself a kind of identi-kit picture of the Loch Ness Monster. Convinced of its existence, he mounted a one-man expedition to Loch Ness in April 1960. He took three moving-picture cameras and probably a better knowledge of 'Nessie', as the Monster was now nicknamed, than anyone else in the world. He had undertaken a formidable task. Loch Ness is twenty-two-and-a-half miles long and has an average width of one mile. It covers an area of 14,000 acres and, at its deepest, goes down to 754 feet.

Right at the start, Mr. Dinsdale seemed to be in luck. He saw what he took to be two sinuous grey humps rising out of the surface of the Loch and hurriedly made his camera ready. Then he focused his binoculars on the object—and found it to be a floating log! Doubters have suggested that many sightings of 'Nessie' have been sightings of floating logs. They point out that the waterlogged trunk of a tree can float up to the surface with the aid of gases produced as it decays. Once the gas escapes, the log sinks again, adding to the illusion of a monster submerging.

But on 23rd April, Mr. Dinsdale made up for his earlier disappointment. He saw what he took to be the back of the monster sticking out of the water, and took a moving-picture of it as it swam away. On 13th June, he appeared on the BBCtv programme, Panorama, with it. It showed the humped back beginning to submerge and a pattern of movement on the waters of the Loch as the creature swam away.

Later Mr. Dinsdale's film was studied by the Joint Air Reconnaissance Intelligence Centre which interprets aerial photographs for the Royal Air Force. They enlarged the film twenty times and reported: 'The assumption is that it is not a surface vessel. One can presumably rule out the idea that it is any sort of submarine vessel, which leaves the conclusion that it is probably an animate object.' They worked out that whatever this object was, it was ninety-two feet long and travelled at ten miles an hour.

Yet Mr. Dinsdale's film was not regarded as conclusive evidence for the existence of the Loch Ness Monster, and the quest for it goes on.

In recent years, more scientific interest has been shown in the possibility that the monster exists and, in 1960, thirty students from Oxford and Cambridge universities took part in an expedition. They used cameras and echo-sounding equipment. They reported seeing what appeared to be the Monster's back moving through the water, and they obtained echoes from an unidentified object. But they were able to reach no conclusion as to whether the Monster exists or not.

That same year, on 19th September, Torquil MacLeod reported one of the most remarkable sightings. He said that he had been able to study the Loch Ness Monster on shore through binoculars for several minutes and he produced a detailed description of it. He said that the length overall of the creature was fifty-one feet. It had a large, grey-black body with a long neck. On this he was unable to make out a head. It had two pairs of flippers, at the front and rear of its body.

In 1962, the Loch Ness Phenomena Investigation Bureau was set up at Inverness to make a serious study of 'Nessie'. In 1967, Clem Lister Skelton, who worked for the Bureau, claimed eight sightings himself. He said, 'The chances of seeing her are not very good. We've averaged a sighting for every 350 man-hours of watching over the past five years. Of course, we're not sure if we always see the same one.' He added that there might be as many as thirty monsters in the Loch!

In September 1969, amidst a great deal of publicity, Independent Television News carried out 'a fourteen-day concentrated search for the Loch Ness Monster—the most sophisticated and scientific expedition ever mounted in the Loch'.

It had taken I.T.N. nine months to organise their expedition. It included echo-sounding equipment, a camera hung under a captive balloon which took pictures from time to time, and a midget submarine. Said I.T.N.: 'With over fifty men and women operating the latest under-water devices and keeping watch on cameras placed strategically around the loch, (the expedition) has the best chance to date of finding the answer' to the mystery of the Loch Ness Monster.

I.T.N. were not relying upon a chance encounter with the Monster. Some echo-sounding equipment was placed to provide a vertical curtain through the waters of the Loch. Other equipment was set to scan the surface. The Monster was to be tempted within range with food consisting of anchovy, blood meal and gelatine.

The Monster was believed to shy away from noise; so under-water noise-makers were to be mounted on launches and driven towards the echo-sounding equipment. It was hoped that the Monster would be driven before these launches.

In spite of everything, the I.T.N. expedition drew a blank. The report from Loch Ness on 27th September was disappointing. 'The I.T.N. search for "Nessie" is drawing to a damp—and probably inconclusive—close. The twenty-four miles of the loch have been scoured as never before. The two sonar teams have kept their day and night vigil in vain. Not once did their screens show even the briefest orange "blip" which would indicate something unusual stirring in the loch.'

Mike Fidell of the I.T.N. expedition believed that their sonar search was ninety-nine per cent effective. The expedition left him seriously doubting the existence of the Monster. He said, 'I don't see how it could have escaped our sonar beams.'

So the mystery of the Loch Ness Monster remains. According to Independent Television News, more than three thousand people have reported seeing the Monster over the years. Were they all in error?—wrongly interpreting what they saw, or victims of their imagination?

To date, no evidence has been produced to prove beyond a reasonable doubt the existence of the Monster. Yet many people believe that it exists, and the search for it goes on.

If the Monster does exist, what can it be? A number of ideas have been put forward. These include: a huge, unknown type of long-necked seal; a monstrous member of the newt family; a huge water-worm; a gigantic eel; a form of plesiosaur.

The plesiosaur is a dinosaur thought to be extinct since the cretaceous period over seventy million years ago. Plesiosaurs lived in the seas of Europe and descriptions of them have features in common with descriptions of the Loch Ness Monster. 'The plesiosaurs as a group were characterised by big paddle-shaped flippers which they used more or less like oars, and they were anything but graceful in their appearance. Some of the long-necked forms have been aptly described as resembling nothing so much as a snake pulled through the body of a turtle.'

In prehistoric times, the seas covered the area where present-day Scottish lochs lie. Is it possible that, when the seas retreated, marine creatures were left behind and have somehow managed to live on to the present day?

If this idea seems far-fetched, think of this. The coelacanth was a fish found as a fossil and believed to have become extinct 250-million years ago. In 1938 one was found alive swimming in the Indian Ocean, and since then many more have been captured.

THE LOST EXPEDITION—A MYSTERY SOLVED

'I AM ANXIOUS to make a balloon voyage over the ice. In fact, I am willing to make an attempt to reach the North Pole itself by balloon.'

The speaker was a tall man with a stern face and a heavy moustache, a forty-two-year-old Swedish engineer named Salomon August Andrée. At the time he was speaking, in 1894, no one had ever reached the North Pole. The farthest north anyone had ever been was eighty-three degrees twenty minutes—about five hundred miles from the North Pole. But Andrée spoke confidently about his idea. He had given it a great deal of thought. He had visited the United States and there met the famous balloonist John Wise and discussed ballooning with him. Afterwards he had bought a balloon which he called *Svea*.

In *Svea*, Andrée made a trial flight of twenty-five miles and went up to nearly 11,000 feet. Now he was talking to another expert—an explorer named Erik Nordenskjold. Nordenskjold was impressed by Andrée's ideas. 'Get your plans down on paper,' he said. 'Keep in touch with me. If I can help you, I will certainly do so.'

So it came about that, on 13th February, 1895, Andrée stood up to address a public meeting in the hall of the Swedish Geographical Society in Stockholm. The chairman at the meeting was Erik Nordenskjold.

He was a famous man, and he had introduced the unknown Andrée to his audience.

It was just as well, for otherwise they might not have listened to the stern-faced engineer. To many of them, what he said was preposterous.

'We must find a different, more modern and more efficient way of reaching the North Pole than the sledge drawn by dogs or men. The broken nature of the ice encountered makes such pedestrian progress slow and difficult, and, incidentally, the polar drift will tend to carry such an expedition away from its objective. Now I claim that this more modern and more efficient method of reaching the Pole is, in the present state of science, the balloon. Yes, gentlemen, the balloon. Supported by favourable winds it will allow us to reach the Pole and return in safety.'

As Andrée talked it became plain that he had worked out his ideas carefully. He knew the size of the balloon he wanted and the amount of food and supplies needed, and he had worked out how long his historic flight was likely to take. He invited questions and answered them confidently. When, at last, he sat down the audience clapped enthusiastically. They believed in Andrée's ideas.

For his expedition, Andrée needed a bigger balloon than had ever been built before, in addition to food and supplies for three months and various scientific instruments and other equipment. To pay for all this he estimated that he needed 130,000 crowns. He was ready to spend all his own money on the expedition but this was not much. He had to obtain the rest from other people.

The King of Sweden gave a large sum of money and so did several rich people. Soon Andrée had his 130,000 crowns, and he sent plans of the balloon he wanted to designers in several countries. In the end he chose a firm in Paris to build the balloon. It had a capacity of

63,000 cubic feet, and it took six months to build. Andrée named it *Ornen* which means Eagle.

Meantime, Andrée was making a study of the winds that blow in the Arctic—as much as was known of them, that is. He had decided to set out on his expedition from Danes Island near Spitzbergen in Norway. Spitzbergen lies well inside the Arctic Circle.

From there it is about eight hundred miles to the North Pole. Andrée hoped to have a 20 m.p.h. wind blowing him towards the Pole and intended to fly right on across the polar ice-cap to Alaska.

No one had ever made such a long flight in a balloon. But then, no one had ever had a balloon like Andrée's. He was confident that he would complete the flight. He had invented a system for steering the balloon using long ropes which would trail over the ice or in the sea. If needed, these ropes could be reeled in to add to the weight in the balloon.

Andrée had chosen two companions to accompany him on his flight. One was Dr. Nils Strindberg, a scientist aged twenty-four. He stood over six feet and weighed more than thirteen stones. The other was Professor Nils Ekholm, an expert on weather.

In the summer of 1896, Andrée took the balloon *Ornen* to Danes Island by ship. Soon, all was ready and Andrée only wanted a southerly wind to blow. Then he could set out. He believed that such a wind blew steadily in the Arctic in the summer.

Each day brought new hope; but Andrée waited in vain for a southerly wind. Every day the wind came from the north. It was more likely to blow Andrée and his companions back to Sweden than over the top of the world.

On 17th August, 1896, with winter approaching, Andrée sadly dismantled the balloon and returned to Sweden.

Back home, Andrée found that he was no longer a popular public figure. All along some people had said that his idea of flying to the North Pole was a wild one. Now these people attacked his plans. To make matters worse, Professor Ekholm withdrew from the expedition. He said, 'I have come to the conclusion that the balloon is not capable of flying to the Pole.'

Yet Andrée refused to be dismayed. To take Ekholm's place he chose a young engineer, Knut Fraenkel, and he returned to Danes Island in the spring of 1897. He still believed that a southerly wind blew for part of the year in the Arctic and he had made up his mind not to miss it this time.

By the middle of June, all was ready again, and once more Andrée was waiting for the southerly wind. Ten days passed. No change. The wind blew steadily from the north. June gave way to July. Sometimes the wind blew from the north, sometimes from the west. Never from the south.

On 6th–7th July, a gusty wind began to blow from the south. It drove the balloon against the wall of its hangar and caused some damage but it also raised hopes. However, Andrée shook his head. 'This wind won't last,' he said. He was right. Soon the north wind was blowing again.

In the early hours of 11th July, gusts of wind began to blow from the south. They were reported at once to Andrée and he got up immediately. He had set up a small observatory on the island, and he hurried there to study the details of the weather. He found that the wind direction was not south but south-south-west. Its speed at ground level was fifteen to twenty miles an hour.

Were conditions right for take off? Andrée decided that this needed thinking about. In the meantime, preparations were begun in case he made up his mind to do so.

By nine o'clock, all was ready. The sky had become clear overhead with some clouds massing in the distance. Andrée spoke to Strindberg and Fraenkel. 'What do you think?' he asked. 'Should we set out?'

Strindberg did not hesitate. 'Yes,' he replied. 'I think we ought to take the chance.'

Fraenkel was not sure at first but, finally, he agreed.

Andrée announced that they were ready to take off. But he admitted that he was agreeing to do so 'without much conviction.'

The black envelope of the balloon rose from the ground. The gondola was fixed in place below.

The captain of the ship that had brought Andrée to Danes Island was in charge of the ground party. Andrée shook hands with him and gave him two messages, one for the King of Sweden, the other for a newspaper called the *Aftonbladet*. The messages announced the departure of the expedition. After this, Strindberg, Fraenkel and Andrée climbed into the gondola.

Men were holding the balloon down with ropes. Now Andrée called to them. 'One, two, three. Let her go!' The ropes were released and the balloon rose into the air. From Andrée and his companions came a shout, 'Long live Sweden!' From the ground party came a ragged burst of cheering and cries of 'Good luck!'

The balloon moved slowly out to sea, steering ropes trailing in the water. It had not gained much height. 'What's he doing?' cried someone. 'They'll be in the water in a minute.'

The balloon carried ballast in the form of sacks of sand, and, at last, nine were tossed out one after another. But the balloon didn't rise. It was drifting slowly downwards towards the water and, minutes later, it struck the sea with a great splash.

At once two boats were pushed out and men began rowing to the aid of Andrée and his companions. But their help was not needed. Suddenly the balloon rose majestically into the air and headed northwards with the wind. The watchers estimated that it was travelling at 20 m.p.h.

As the balloon sailed into the distance, the ground party turned away. Then someone noticed a mass of ropes lying on the ground. It was part of Andrée's steering system. The ropes had been caught in something on the ground and had been torn off when the balloon took

off. So Andrée's hopes of steering the balloon were ended. He was entirely at the mercy of whatever winds might blow.

Andrée had taken with him in the balloon thirty-two carrier pigeons. He planned to set these birds free with messages from time to time. He was not sure whether they would find their way back to Denmark. But he was hoping that they might.

On 16th July, between one and two o'clock in the morning, Captain Ole Hansen of the whaler *Alken* heard the flapping of wings in the shrouds above his ship. He looked up and saw a strange bird which seemed

to be exhausted. Hansen promptly shot the bird. It fell
into the sea and he didn't think it worth lowering a
boat to recover it.

Later that same day, the *Alken* came alongside
another whaler. Hansen told the other captain about

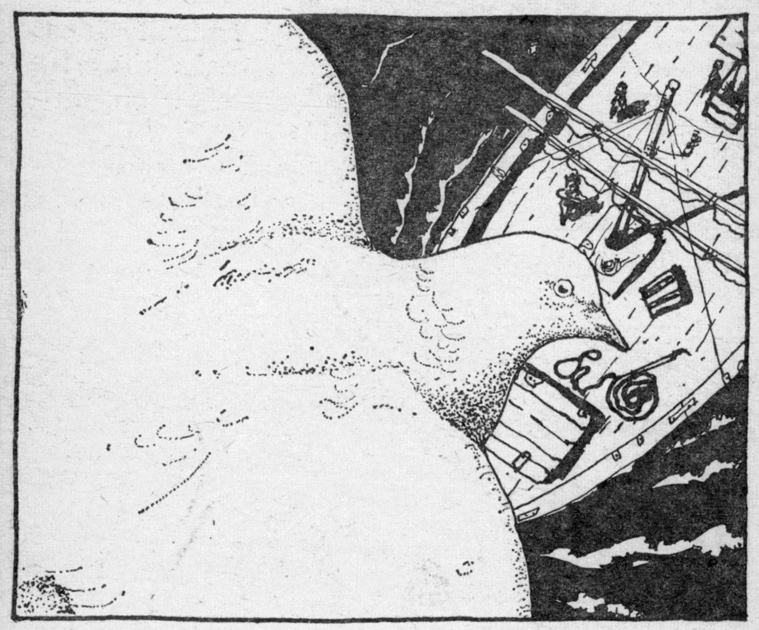

the strange bird he had shot. 'I believe it was a ptarmi-
gan,' he said.

'Do you think it might have been one of Andrée's
pigeons?' asked the other captain.

'I didn't know he'd started.'

The more Hansen thought about the bird, the more
he worried whether it might have been a pigeon carrying a message from Andrée. In the end he made up his
mind to sail back to the place where he had shot the
bird. He turned the *Alken* through one hundred and
eighty degrees.

The look-out was warned to keep his eyes open for the

body of the bird drifting in the grey waters and, incredibly, he spotted it. Quickly a boat was lowered and the body was recovered.

The bird *was* a carrier pigeon. Under its wing was a small tube containing waxed paper, and on the paper was this message: 'From the Andrée Polar Expedition to the *Aftonbladet*, July 13 at 12.30 hours. Position: Latitude 82.02 North; Longitude (Greenwich) 15.15. This is the third message despatched by pigeon. All is well aboard. Making good speed.'

In time, the message was passed on to the *Aftonbladet* and the news was published in the newspaper. After that people waited eagerly for further messages. But there were none.

The winter of 1897–8 came and passed. People returning from the Arctic such as whaling skippers were immediately asked: 'Have you heard anything of Andrée?' The answer was always the same. No one had heard anything.

If the balloon had come down on the ice, Andrée and his companions could have lived through the Arctic winter. They were well equipped with supplies and food. With this in mind, four separate expeditions set out to look for the missing explorers. All of them returned empty-handed.

On 14th May, 1899, fishermen in Kolla Fjord on the north coast of Iceland found a buoy containing a message. The message said: 'This buoy was dropped from Andrée's balloon at 10.55 hours G.M.T. in the evening of July 11, 1897. Latitude approximately 82 degrees, Longitude 25 degrees Greenwich.' The buoy had been in the water for 672 days before it was found.

In itself, the message told little. But some people thought that the dropping of the buoy was significant. It seemed to indicate that Andrée was dropping overboard other things beyond his ballast. In other words, the balloon was losing height to a dangerous extent.

This fact seemed to be confirmed on 27th August, 1900. On that date the buoy Andrée had intended to drop at the North Pole was found on the shore at Finmark in Norway. It had been drifting in the sea for perhaps 1,142 days.

The buoy was damaged and experts studied it carefully. It had been attached to the gondola of the balloon by a cord. The experts said that it had probably been shaken free 'as a result of some hard shock.'

From the outset of the expedition, Andrée had been aware of one great danger facing them. In bad weather over the polar regions the fabric of the balloon would become wet. The great size of the balloon meant that this wetness would amount to a considerable weight. Such a weight might force the balloon down on the ice. Crashing on to the ice might have shaken the buoy free.

At this stage, there was a tremendous amount of guessing about what might have happened to Andrée and his companions and, at the same time, many rumours spread. At one time a mysterious balloon was said to have been seen in the sky over Alaska. Then it was reported, falsely, that the bodies of the three men had been found in a forest near the Yenisei River in Siberia. They were supposed to have been murdered by Eskimos.

Another search party went out to the eastern coast of Greenland thinking that the balloon might have come down there. Two hundred and fifty miles of the coastline was searched. The search produced nothing.

In 1900, the famous Norwegian polar explorer, Fridtjof Nansen spoke about Andrée at the Geographical Congress in Berlin. He said, 'Alas there is now no hope whatever that we shall ever see those unfortunate explorers again. They are, let us face the fact, lost for ever.'

None knew conditions in the Arctic better than Nansen. He himself had spent five months marching five hundred miles across the polar wastes. If he held out no hope for Andrée and his companions then assuredly, there was no hope.

Time passed. The mystery remained but interest in it died down. Yet in the Ethnographical Museum in Stockholm there were permanent reminders of the ill-fated expedition in the form of five exhibits. They were two messages, two rusty buoys and a stuffed carrier pigeon. Persons seeing them could not fail to ask themselves tantalising questions: What happened to Andrée, Strindberg and Fraenkel? Were they the first men to reach the North Pole?

On the face of it, it seemed as if these two questions might never be answered. The three men had vanished over the Arctic and there their story seemed to end. But it did not end. The solution of the mystery was waiting to be discovered.

*   *   *

White Island lies inside the Arctic Circle. It is usually hemmed in with pack-ice; so it is not often visited. But, in August 1930, a Norwegian ship, the *Bratvaag*, found open water close by and dropped anchor. A party of sailors went ashore to hunt seals. Suddenly one of them called out in amazement. 'I say,' he cried. 'Just look at this!' He was holding up the lid of a cooking pot.

'I wonder where that can have come from,' said another of the men. 'I have never heard of anyone landing on White Island.'

The sailors looked to see if there was anything else to be found. Soon they discovered, buried in the snow, the remains of a camp and the body of a man. They also found a canvas bag bearing the legend 'Andrée's Polar Expedition 1896'.

The sailors had solved the thirty-three-year-old mystery of what had happened to Salomon Andrée, for the body was his. This they guessed from finding the letter 'A' on his jacket.

Later, men from the *Bratvaag* also found the body of Strindberg and various other items belonging to the expedition including a canvas boat. The captain took

the two bodies on board and set out at once for Sweden.

The news, when it broke, created a sensation and at once a party of newspaper-men set out for White Island in a sealing boat. The leader of this party, Knut Stubbendorff, carried out a careful search of the island. He found Knut Fraenkel's body, log-books kept by Strindberg and Andrée's diary and his box camera. The logbook and the diary told almost the whole story.

Drifting through thick Arctic fog, the silk envelope of the balloon had become saturated with water and the weight of this had forced them down on the ice early in the morning of 14th July. They had reached eighty-two degrees fifty-six minutes north having covered three hundred miles from Danes Island in sixty-six hours fourteen minutes.

The balloon was not damaged in landing and the three men unloaded food and equipment and set out to march to the nearest land. That lay two hundred and sixteen miles to the south across the pack-ice.

Pulling sledges loaded with food, they were in good spirits. Each day Andrée made notes of such things as the temperature and the winds. He thought that these notes might be useful to other people who tried to reach the North Pole.

He also worked out their exact position from the sun by day and the stars at night. Soon he realised that they were making poor progress. While they were walking southwards, the ice they were walking on was drifting to the north.

For two months they pressed on, adding to their food supplies by shooting polar bears and seals. Then winter began to close in. 'We must make camp for the winter,' said Andrée.

They started to build a hut of ice thinking that they were on an island. But they were on an iceberg and, one morning, it broke up with a tremendous crack. Their hut collapsed and food and equipment fell into the water.

They rescued what they could and made their way over the ice to White Island. There they set up camp and began to build a hut of stone. Thirty-three years later their bodies were found at this spot.

The last entry in Andrée's diary was dated 17th October, 1897. That was ninety-eight days after the expedition had set out in the balloon from Danes Island.

Andrée's camera contained plates in good condition. From these plates photographs were later printed. One showed the wreck of the *Ornen* down on the ice. Another showed Andrée standing with his rifle beside a dead polar bear.

Why Andrée and his companions died remains a mystery. Stores of food were found near their last camp and the oil stove was in working order. So they evidently did not die of hunger or cold.

In Sweden, the explorers had never been forgotten. Their bodies were taken home in 1930 in the warship *Svenskund* which had sailed with Andrée to Danes Island thirty-three years before. At Gothenburg, 75,000 people saw wreaths carried aboard the warship and then, escorted by other naval vessels, she sailed along the coast of Sweden to the capital, Stockholm. As the flotilla passed, the bells of the churches along the shore were rung in memory of three very brave men.

On 24TH JUNE, 1947, Kenneth Arnold, a young American businessman, was flying his private aeroplane above the Cascade Mountains in Washington. As he drew near Mount Rainier he saw nine circular objects moving at high speed pass twenty-five miles away. There was a Douglas D.C.4 airliner in the sky at the same time, and Arnold thought that each of the objects was slightly smaller than this aircraft. The objects flew 'as if they were linked together,' swerving in and out of the high peaks of the mountains with 'flipping, erratic movements.'

On landing, Arnold described what he had seen. He told a newspaper reporter that the objects 'flew like a saucer would if you skipped it across the water.' His words provided a name for the objects he had seen. Kenneth Arnold was the first observer reported to have seen flying saucers.

Within a few weeks of the report of what Arnold had seen, reports of similar sightings came from various parts of the world—from Canada, Australia, England and Iran.

From the start, there was a great deal of guessing about what the flying saucers might be. An American newspaper reporter stated that the saucers were, in fact, a new, secret type of aircraft, 'a combination of helicopter and fast jet plane'. This proved to be incorrect. In 1947, a so-called 'cold war' was in progress between the

United States and the Soviet Union and one famous
newspaper writer suggested that the saucers were a new
type of spy aircraft sent out from Russia. Another idea
was that the flying saucers came from outer space, sent
by beings from another world.

As is the way of newspapers, they tended to carry
stories of flying saucers for the next few months, and
many of the stories were either false or mistaken. But
some of the stories were genuine enough to raise seriously in the minds of people in authority the question:
Do flying saucers exist? In time, the term 'flying saucer'
has given way to the more scientific one 'unidentified
flying object', and for over two decades from 1947 a
great deal of investigation was carried out into U.F.O.s
in the United States.

An expert from the U.S. Army Air Force soon called
to question Kenneth Arnold about what he had seen.

The young man told his story quite clearly. At about three o'clock in the afternoon, he noticed a bright flash of light in the sky. Then he saw the nine objects. He said, 'I could see their outline quite plainly against the snow as they approached the mountain. They flew very close to the mountain-tops, flying like geese in a diagonal chainlike line, as if they were linked together. They were flat like a pie pan and so shiny that they reflected the sun like a mirror.' Arnold estimated that the objects were flying at 9,500 feet and travelling at something like 1,700 miles an hour—three times faster than any aircraft known in 1947.

The expert returned from seeing Arnold and handed in his report. He believed that Arnold was telling the truth. He said, 'If he made up that story, he is in the wrong business. He should be writing science fiction for a living.'

On the other hand, it was possible to pick holes in Arnold's story. Arnold had estimated the size of the objects he saw as about fifty feet long. 'At a distance of twenty-five miles,' said some experts, 'he wouldn't have seen something that size.' Experts also questioned his estimate of the speed. 'If the objects were travelling that fast, he wouldn't have seen them,' they said.

In the end, the experts provided an explanation of what Arnold had seen. It was a mirage caused by 'unusual atmospheric conditions.' This was an explanation that Arnold would not accept. He said, 'I am absolutely certain of what I saw.'

By this time, it was widely known that sightings of unidentified flying objects were not new. Reports of such objects date back three thousand years. Some people include among these reports of fiery chariots, glowing lights and strange clouds which are mentioned in the Bible.

In the early days of the Roman Empire, a round object that looked like a globe or shield was said to have been seen moving across the sky. On another occasion a fiery globe, brighter than the sun, was reported to have been seen, first falling towards the earth and then rising again.

In A.D. 80, Roman soldiers in Scotland said that they saw bright flames in the sky one winter's night and something that looked like a ship moving across the sky on several occasions. Eighteen years later, something that looked like a burning shield was seen to pass across the sky in Rome.

Similar stories were told in the Middle Ages. Matthew of Paris recorded that what appeared to be a very bright star passed over England one evening and vanished in the north. A few years later, he stated, monks at St. Albans saw a large vessel in the sky like one of the ships of their time.

Robert of Reading recorded that, in 1323, a fiery shape was seen crossing the sky over England and observers noted that, when a bright red flame burst from it, it travelled faster.

Other Medieval writers described bright lights, balls, discs and strange shapes that were seen in the sky.

In 1644, sailors on a Spanish merchant ship saw several glowing objects in the night sky. For a time the objects broke formation and moved in a haphazard fashion. Then they fell into formation again and sped out of sight.

John Evelyn, the famous diarist, described a 'shining cloud' seen over England in March 1643. He wrote: 'I must not forget what amazed us exceedingly the night before, namely, a shining cloud in the air, in shape resembling a sword, the point reaching to the north; it was as bright as the moon, the rest of the sky being serene. It began about eleven at night, and vanished not till about one, being seen by all the south of England.'

In 1742, a large brightly-lighted object shaped like a cylinder was reported to have been seen over London.

In 1833, a brightly-lighted hooklike shape was seen over Ohio in the United States and that same year a large, glowing object was seen in the sky by people living in Niagara Falls, New York. In 1846, a big disc was seen flying over Lowell, Massachusetts.

On 1st August 1871, an astronomer named Coggia saw a strange red object in the sky over Marseilles, France.

On 17th November, 1882, an astronomer named E. W. Maunder watching the heavens from the Royal Observatory, Greenwich, saw a great circular disc of greenish light. Other people saw the object the same night. They described it as being cigar-shaped, like a torpedo or like a spindle. The object was in plain sight of Mr. Maunder for two minutes.

In 1885, two ladies in Bermuda, Mrs. Adelina Bassett and Mrs. L. Lowell saw a triangular object in the sky. It was 'about the size of a pilot-boat mainsail, with chains attached to the bottom of it.'

In spring 1897, newspapers in the United States reported many cases of unidentified flying objects being seen. People in Omaha, Nebraska, saw a brightly-lighted object that was too big to be a balloon. A day later a farmer in Sioux City, Iowa, claimed to have been caught by a hook dangling from a similar object and dragged along the ground. A week later people in Omaha once more saw a brightly-lighted object in the sky and this time it seemed to have a steel body and be twelve to fifteen feet long. Reports of sightings followed from Mt. Carroll (Illinois), Wausau (Wisconsin), Washington, D.C. and places in Texas and Virginia. Some of the objects seen were said to be cigar-shaped and to have flashed red, green and white lights.

In 1912, Charles Tilden Smith in Chisbury, Wiltshire, saw two triangular objects in the sky. Smith said that he had studied the skies for years and never seen anything like them before.

In January and February 1913, 'unknown airships' were seen at various times over many different places in Britain. Whatever they were, they gave out a great deal of light. Some people later believed these U.F.O.s had a simple explanation. Zeppelins were used to bomb Britain in World War One (1914–18) and it is thought that they might have been sent to spy on Britain just before the war.

In July 1938 a U.F.O. flew over New York. It shone brilliantly and gave forth a sound described as 'a great swish', 'a persistent hiss' and 'a faraway roar'. It was lost to sight when it fell below the horizon, possibly falling into the sea. Experts declared that the object was a large meteorite but not everyone who saw it agreed. A lecturer at the Planetarium in New York said it was like 'a rocket with a brilliant exhaust'. Another witness said it was like 'a giant Roman Candle'.

In the years before World War Two there were frequent reports of aircraft crashing into the sea without leaving a trace and *without any known aircraft being missing*.

Study of the files of newspapers and magazines indicates a considerable amount of interest in U.F.O.s for over a century.

Not all reports of flying saucers are genuine; not all are worthy of serious study—the stories are too vague. But some reports stand out from all the rest and defy an explanation. Such a report occurred on 7th January, 1948. People living in Maysville, Kentucky, saw what seemed to be a curious aircraft pass over the town, and reports of what they had seen were passed to the state Highway Patrol. The Highway Patrol got in touch with a U.S. Air Force base at Godman, near Louisville, to see if they knew anything about the aircraft. The answer was, 'No,' but the men in the control tower at the airfield said that they would watch out for it.

Some time afterwards, an aircraft control officer saw

something above the airfield. It was a large object and it looked metallic. It appeared to be hovering over the airfield.

At this time, four F-51 fighter aircraft of the National Guard were approaching the airfield. The control tower at Godman called their leader, Captain Thomas Mantell. They asked if he would help to identify the strange aircraft.

One of the F-51s was short of fuel but the other three set out to investigate. At first, they saw nothing but, at 15,000 feet, Mantell saw something above him. The control tower asked him what it looked like and he replied, 'It looks metallic and tremendous in size. Now it's starting to climb.' Seconds later Mantell said, 'I'm climbing to 20,000 feet.' After that, nothing more was heard from him.

The other two F-51s returned to base but Captain Mantell's aircraft had vanished. The wreckage of it was later found forty miles from Godman. Captain Mantell was dead.

Mantell's death gave rise to all kinds of wild rumours. It was suggested that his aircraft had been blown to pieces when it drew near the U.F.O. Investigators of the U.S. Air Force told another story. The F-51 had originally set out on a low-level mission and was not carrying oxygen tanks. But at 20,000 feet, the pilot would have needed oxygen. Presumably Captain Mantell flew too high and blacked out leaving his plane out of control.

The question remained: What was the object seen over Godman that day? The most likely explanation seemed to be a huge high-level balloon called a Skyhook. These balloons were being used on research by the U.S. Navy. But it was never proved that a Skyhook balloon could have been in the area of Godman on 7th January, 1948.

On the night of 24th July, 1948. Clarence S. Chiles

and John B. Whitted were flying a Douglas D.C.3 of
Eastern Airlines from Houston, Texas to Atlanta,
Georgia. Near Montgomery, Alabama, a brilliantly
glowing object flew towards them, and then pulled up
and disappeared into clouds. The two men described
the object later as a cigar-shaped, wingless aircraft
about 100 feet long. It had a smooth surface and two
rows of lighted windows. The bottom of it was lit by a
dark-blue glow and flames came out of it at the rear for
a distance of about fifty feet.

It was 2.45 a.m. and most of the passengers were
asleep; so they did not see the U.F.O. But at 1.45 a.m. a
bright light was seen to pass over Robbins Air Force
Base at Macon, Georgia, and at 2.45 a.m. two military
pilots flying some miles from Montgomery saw what appeared to be a bright shooting star in the distance.

These sightings were investigated by the U.S. Air
Force. They checked aircraft in the area and found that
none had been flying near the D.C.3. But they discovered that, that week, a large number of meteors
had been seen over the South-East of the United States.
The bright light seen at Macon and that seen by the
two military pilots were probably meteors and it
seemed as if what Chiles and Whitted had seen was
probably one, too.

Not everyone was ready to accept this explanation.
This was because Chiles and Whitted were reliable wit-
nesses and both agreed upon what they saw. Their case
is regarded as a U.F.O. classic—a sighting which has
not been explained away.

Another classic sighting occurred in the evening of
1st October, 1948. Lieutenant George F. Gorman of
the North Dakota Air National Guard was coming in
to land his F-51 on the airfield at Fargo. The control
tower told him that a Piper Cub was to land before him.
Gorman picked out the lights of the Piper Cub below
him. But he also saw another moving light. At once he

called the tower and asked if there was another aircraft in the landing pattern. The tower said that there wasn't. One of the ground control officers looked through the window and saw a clear white light moving towards the north.

At this point, Gorman called again. He said that he was going to follow the light to find out what it was. Watched, at first, through binoculars from the tower, Gorman chased the moving light from 1,000 up to 14,000 feet. During this time, the light sometimes changed direction and flew towards Gorman's aircraft. Twenty-five miles from Fargo it suddenly shot upwards and disappeared.

The U.S. Air Force investigated. Four people besides Gorman had seen the light, two ground control officers, the pilot of the Piper Cub and a passenger in it. In spite of his nearness to it, Gorman had only seen a round white light measuring six to eight inches across. But he was convinced that the light was being guided by someone.

The explanation put forward by the investigators was simple. A lighted weather balloon had been set free from Fargo that evening. The wind would have carried it over the airfield. What they did not explain was why Gorman, an experienced pilot who knew about weather balloons, had not recognised what he was chasing. Nor did they explain the balloon's abrupt changes of direction.

On 3rd September, 1965, Norman Muscarello, a young man living in Exeter, New Hampshire, was walking home at about two o'clock in the morning. A few miles from the town he saw, above a field, what appeared to be a round object about eighty to ninety feet in diameter. Around the rim of the object were bright, flickering red lights. Muscarello's reaction was immediate. He dived into a ditch at the roadside. He watched the strange object move away and then ran into the road-

way to stop a passing car. He was given a lift to the
police station in Exeter.

He told his story at the police station. The officer in
charge thought that the young man might be having a
joke but he decided to call in a patrol car. The officer

who drove in, Eugene Bertrand, had a strange story of
his own to tell. An hour earlier he had found a terri-
fied woman in a parked car. She said that she had been
followed by a large flying object with flashing red lights.

Bertrand drove Muscarello back to the field, and
there both of them saw the mysterious object. It appeared to hover about one hundred feet above the
ground. Bertrand called in over his radio, 'I've seen it
myself!' and a second patrol car driven by David Hunt
arrived at the scene. He, too, saw the U.F.O.

In the weeks that followed, many other people reported seeing U.F.O.s in the region of Exeter. The sighting by Muscarello was investigated by the U.S. Air

Force. They put forward two possible explanations: 1. Aircraft of Strategic Air Command were carrying out a big operation in the area that night; perhaps the U.F.O. was one of these aircraft. 2. A trick of the atmosphere caused by layers of warm air might have made stars and planets appear to move in unusual formations.

Neither explanation covered all the facts in the case, and the object was officially classified as unidentified. Students of U.F.O. lore list it as a classic.

Since flying saucers first came into the news, many people in various countries have reported making contact with beings from them. Official investigators have never treated such stories seriously. No proof of them has ever been forthcoming.

An amateur astronomer named George Adamski claimed to have met men from other planets many times in the 1950s. Adamski said that he talked with them using sign language and made journeys in their space-craft—including a trip around the Moon. He produced photographs to support his stories but he was unable to prove that the photographs were genuine.

Over the years, many photographs of objects said to be flying saucers have been produced by various people. Some of them have been shown to be fakes. The others have not been accepted as genuine pictures of U.F.O.s beyond a reasonable doubt.

Another report of seeing men from outer space came in April 1964 from Sergeant Lonnie Zamora of the Socorro (New Mexico) Police Force. Zamora was on patrol outside the city when he heard a roar and saw flames in the sky. He set out to investigate.

He left the road and began driving across country along a gravel path. This took him up a steep hill. By the time he reached the top of the hill, the flames had vanished. On the other side he saw something shiny about one hundred and fifty to two hundred yards away. It appeared to be an upturned car. Zamora stopped. He saw two figures in white overalls standing close to the shiny object.

Zamora drove nearer and got out of his car. As he did so, there came a loud roar like the one he had heard before. Blue and orange flames sprouted from under the shiny object. It rose from the ground and sped away into the distance.

Soon afterwards Sergeant Sam Chavez joined Zamora. The two men found charred brush near where the object had been standing and then Chavez noticed four shallow holes in the ground. They were twelve to fourteen inches long and one–two inches deep. Such marks could have been made by the landing pads of a flying machine.

The Deputy Sheriff of Socorro, an F.B.I. agent and an Army captain from a nearby post arrived on the scene. They inspected it closely. Photographs were taken.

Later experts from the U.S. Air Force carried out an investigation. Their aim was to show what the unidentified flying object might be.

They were unable to put forward any likely explanation. Sergeant Zamora's U.F.O. remained unidentified and the mystery remains of the two figures he saw. He described them later as being 'normal in shape, but possibly they were small adults or large kids.' Were these beings from outer space?

From the time Kenneth Arnold saw the first flying saucer, there was concern in the United States, and in February 1948 the U.S. Air Force opened Project Sign. The object of this operation was to investigate serious reports of U.F.O.s. In the following year, two hundred and forty-three sightings were investigated. At the end of that time, the Air Force announced that they were unable to prove or disprove that U.F.O.s were unknown types of aircraft.

In 1949, two hundred and forty-four U.F.O. sightings were investigated. Explanations were found for seventy-seven per cent of them. As a result, the project was dropped. But U.F.O.s were still being seen over the United States and another project had to be started. This was Project Blue Book. It ran from 1950 to 1969 and investigated around 12,000 U.F.O.s. All but a small percentage of them were explained.

What kind of things cause people to report U.F.O.s? More than 2,000 of the U.F.O. sightings turned out to be planets, bright stars, shooting stars and similar things. 1,500 proved to be high-flying aircraft. About eight hundred were man-made satellites. Five hundred were balloons of various kinds. Other sighting reports were caused by hoaxes, flocks of birds, and even clouds.

In the year that Project Blue Book ended, the 'Condon Report' appeared from the University of Colorado —a 1,465 page book entitled Scientific Study of Flying Objects. Scientists at the University had been studying

U.F.O.s since 1966 under Dr. Edward U. Condon. Money for their work amounting to half a million dollars was provided by the United States Air Force and they were able to use information from Project Blue Book. The Report concluded 'Nothing has come from the study of U.F.O.s in the past twenty-one years that has added to scientific knowledge.'

The Condon Report was soon followed by a book by Dr. David Saunders, *UFOs? Yes! Where the Condon Committee Went Wrong*. But neither Project Blue Book nor the Condon Report denied that U.F.O.s exist. There remain that small percentage of sightings that are unexplained.

What are these U.F.O.s? Are they sent from outer space? Do they contain beings from other worlds? Some people think so. Gabriel Green, president of the Amalgamated Flying Saucer Clubs of America is one of them. He has said: 'Inhabitants of other worlds are holding off their visitation to the troubled earth because they feel that they would either be worshipped as gods or feared as conquerors.'

Perhaps we will have to wait for an explanation of U.F.O.s until we receive it from someone from another world.

ATLANTIS—LOST CONTINENT?

FOR CENTURIES, SOME people have believed that a lost continent lies under the waters of the Atlantic Ocean. The continent has been shown on maps, and more than two thousand books and articles have been written about it. In Victorian times, a Prime Minister of Britain, William Gladstone, wanted to send out an expedition to look for the lost continent. But the Government refused to supply money for the venture.

The name of the lost continent is Atlantis. Did such a place ever exist? If it existed, was it situated in the Atlantic Ocean?

The story of Atlantis as we know it dates back to about 355 B.C. It was told by the Greek philosopher Plato in two books, Timaeus and Critias. In Timaeus, Plato told how the story of Atlantis came to him. It was, he said, told sixty years earlier by a man named Critias. According to Critias, the story had been handed down in his family from Solon the Wise. Solon had told the story one hundred and fifty years earlier still.

Solon had visited the priests of a temple at Sais in Egypt and they had exchanged stories of the past. One of the priests' stories was about the Greek city-state of Athens. Nine thousand years earlier, said the priests, there was a powerful island-state outside the Pillars of Hercules (the Straits of Gibraltar, as we know them today). The island was larger than all the present-day Middle East. This was Atlantis.

Armies from Atlantis invaded the shores of Africa and Europe. They were finally defeated by the city-state of Athens.

Later, there were violent earthquakes and floods and, in a single terrible day and night, the island of Atlantis sank beneath the waves. Where it had been, thick mud made the sea impassable.

In Critias, Plato told a great deal about the island itself. In the middle of it there was a fertile plain surrounded by mountains. On the plain stood the chief city built in the form of a circle. The city measured fifteen miles across with a canal through the middle. The canal connected the sea with the plain and provided water for the plain.

In the city there were palaces, temples and race-tracks. Buildings were decorated with gold, silver, bronze and ivory and a mysterious metal called 'orichalcum'. The ivory came from the tusks of herds of elephants to be found on the island.

Plato told how the people of Atlantis and its neighbouring islands lived and how the islands were run. There were ten kings and they met every fifth or sixth year to talk over the affairs of state. At the start of their meeting, special ceremonies were held, including the sacrifice of a bull.

For hundreds of years, the people of Atlantis were good but then they became greedy and ambitious. Zeus decided to punish them. Zeus, according to the Greeks, was the chief of all the gods. He called the other gods to a meeting in his palace. At this point, Critias comes to a sudden end with the words: 'And when he had assembled them, he spoke thus.' Plato wrote no more. Still, we know from Timaeus what was supposed to have happened to Atlantis.

Plato was a philosopher, not a historian. It was taken for granted in his time and for many years afterwards that he had told the story of Atlantis to make people think. It provided plenty to think about. The way Atlantis was built. The way it was run. The way the people went wrong. The way they were punished by the gods.

The idea of a perfect state was something that Plato had written about before in a book called The Republic. The Republic is such an important book that it is still studied today. But Timaeus and Critias are not considered important. One scholar said of these books, 'In them Plato was resting his mind. He is making up a fairy tale, the most wonderful island that could be imagined.' Yet, by the sixth century, some Roman scholars thought that the story of Atlantis was true.

In the fifteenth century, the age of exploration began with the discovery of America. Then the story of Atlantis began to be told again, and more people believed it. Indeed, map-makers began showing Atlantis on their maps!

In the years that followed, people of many countries began to raise questions and put forward suggestions about Atlantis. Some saw the island as a link between the Old World and the New World of America. Had the Red Indians of North America reached that country by way of Atlantis? Some suggested that the Redskins were descendants of a legendary Welsh prince who had sailed to the West. Others believed that they were the Lost Ten Tribes of Israel. In each case, Atlantis might have provided a stepping stone to the New World. In fact, anthropologists believe that the Redskins are related to the Mongols of Asia. They reached the New World by way of Alaska across the Bering Strait.

The story of Atlantis became further complicated as a result of some study of the writings of the Mayas of Central America. One Abbé Charles-Etienne Brasseur de Bourbourg picked up a book in a library in Madrid. It had been written by a Spanish monk in the sixteenth century, and it included what was supposed to be the

Mayan alphabet—now known to be hopelessly incorrect.

Using this alphabet, Brasseur somehow produced from some Mayan writings an account of the destruction of a land by an earthquake and the eruption of a volcano. He wrongly thought that this land was called Mu—and in the minds of many people, the lost continent of Mu and the lost island of Atlantis promptly became one and the same thing.

One of the people who studied Brasseur's work was Ignatius Donnelly, a member of the United States Senate. Donnelly spent a great deal of time studying in the Library of Congress in Washington and eventually produced a remarkable book—*Atlantis: The Antediluvian World*. Scholars of today can point out that Donnelly's book is a farrago of misinformation. Yet, in its day, it created a sensation. It was this book that caused William Gladstone to suggest that Britain should send an expedition to look for the lost continent.

Donnelly saw Atlantis as the link between the Old World and the New. He made lists of things common to both worlds. For example, marriage and divorce, spears and sails, stories of ghosts and legends of floods. Scholars point out that most of these things are found not only on both sides of the Atlantic Ocean but all over the world.

Donnelly also tried to show that the Mayan alphabet was like Egyptian hieroglyphics. In fact, there is a wide gulf between the two.

Donnelly later produced another book called *The Great Cryptogram*. In this he proved to his own satisfaction that the plays of William Shakespeare were written by Francis Bacon. Scholars took this book even less seriously than Atlantis. One man pointed out that, using Donnelly's methods, you could prove that Shakespeare wrote the Forty-Sixth Psalm in the Bible. The forty-sixth word from the beginning is 'shake'; the forty-sixth from the end is 'spear'.

A French doctor, Augustus Le Plongeon (1826–1908), later claimed that the people of Mu settled in Central America and became the Mayas. Le Plongeon spent a considerable amount of time excavating Mayan

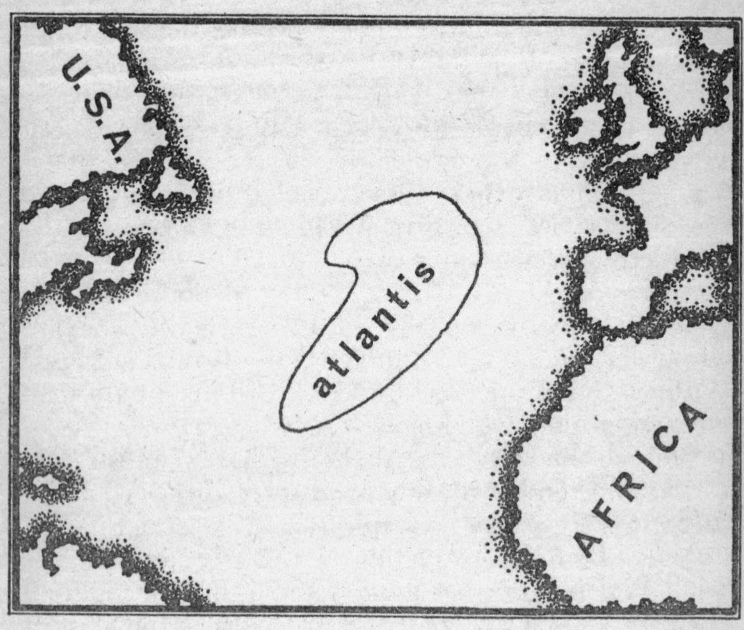

ruins in Yucatan. He said that he was able to piece together the story of Mu from writings of the Mayas—translated with Brasseur's useless alphabet—and some pictures found on walls at Chichen Itza.

According to Le Plongeon, Moo, Queen of Atlantis or Mu, was wanted in marriage by her brothers Coh and Aac. She married Coh, but he was murdered by Aac. After this, the land sank and Moo fled to Egypt. There, using the name Isis, she founded Egyptian civilisation. In the end, she was tracked down and killed by Aac. Meantime, other people from Mu had fled to Central America and become the Mayas.

Not surprisingly, few knowledgeable people took Le Plongeon's account seriously. Nor did they waste much time on the next major account of the lost continent—'How I Discovered Atlantis, the Source of All Civilisation'. This was written by Dr. Paul Schliemann, grandson of the famous Heinrich Schliemann who found the ruins of Troy. It was published in 1912 in New York in a magazine called *American*.

According to Schliemann, his grandfather had left him two things—an envelope containing papers and an ancient vase in the shape of an owl's head. There was a note with the envelope. It said that it must be opened only by a member of the family ready to give up his life to investigating the matter that the papers were about. Paul Schliemann opened the envelope.

Instructions on the first paper told him to break open the owl's-head vase. Paul did so and, inside it, found some square coins of a mixture of platinum, aluminium and silver, and a metal plate. On the plate was written, in Phoenician, 'Issued in the Temple of Transparent Walls'. Presumably these had some connection with Atlantis.

Paul Schliemann said that, among the papers, was one containing an account of the finding of a large bronze vase. It bore the inscription 'From King Cronos of Atlantis'.

Schliemann's article on Atlantis put forward many of Ignatius Donnelly's arguments to show that the island was a link between the Old World and the New. It said that he had found confirmation of the sinking of Atlantis in a curious place—a manuscript four thousand years old produced in Mesopotamia but found by Schliemann in a Buddhist temple in Tibet!

Schliemann's article is now looked upon as a hoax. But, at the time it was published, some people believed it. Those who believed in the myth of Atlantis accepted it as further proof that they were right.

In 1926, 'Colonel' James Churchward, who had done a great deal of travelling around the world, produced a book, *The Lost Continent of Mu*. Churchward claimed to have located something called the 'Naacal Tablets' in a Hindu temple in India (or Tibet, according to a later

book). A priest had kindly translated the tablets for him. They largely confirmed stories put forward by Le Plongeon and Paul Schliemann but had one major difference from previous contributions on the subject of Atlantis. According to Churchward, there was not one lost continent but two—Atlantis in the Atlantic Ocean and Mu in the Pacific.

Can the lost world of Atlantis then be written off, completely, as a fairy tale invented by Plato and added to by others? It would be simple to answer, 'Yes.' Certainly no land like Atlantis could have existed 10,000 years before Plato's time as it was supposed to. At that time, the people of Europe and North Africa were still living in the Stone Age. They were hunters and fishers moving from place to place and using stone tools. They could not have built a city and dug out a canal such as Atlantis was supposed to have.

Nor is it likely that any great land mass should have sunk beneath the sea. Comparatively small areas of land may be suddenly submerged by the sea and a tiny island may be destroyed by an earthquake or the eruption of a volcano. But geologists agree that the destruction of a continent would have to be a slow process taking thousands or even millions of years. They have found no evidence that a continent did, indeed, vanish under the waters of the Atlantic Ocean.

Is there, then, no shred of truth in Plato's story of Atlantis? Did he invent the whole story?

Scholars studying the story of Atlantis in recent years have approached it in this manner. They have wondered whether Plato built his story on a basis of true facts. Some scholars believe that he did.

L. Sprague de Camp and Catherine C. de Camp in *Citadels of Mystery* (1964) list sources of Plato's ideas. That of a land covered by the sea, they say, comes from the fact that, in 426 B.C., the small Greek island of Atalante was submerged after an earthquake, hence the name Atlantis.

The descriptions of the island-state itself, they suggest, are based on accounts of a rich city-state called Tartessos. It stood at the mouth of the River Guadalquivir in South-West Spain, twenty miles north-west of present-day Cadiz.

Tartessos was a centre of trade and silver mining two thousand years before the Birth of Christ. Silver was so common in the city that pigs ate from silver troughs. Greeks traded with Tartessos from about 631 B.C. and looked upon it as the richest city in the West.

Tartessos suddenly vanished about 500 B.C. Nobody

knows what happened to it. Perhaps it was destroyed by enemies from the powerful city of Carthage. Perhaps its harbour silted up and stopped ships from reaching the city to trade. Perhaps it was destroyed by an earthquake.

Tartessos was like Atlantis in many ways. It was in the West (from Greece), it was rich and a centre of trade, it had a broad plain behind the city, and it vanished mysteriously.

More recently, the island of Thera close to the mainland of Greece has been suggested as the source of some of Plato's ideas, together with the island of Crete. In the late Bronze Age, about 1470 B.C., a city built by Minoans on Thera was destroyed by volcanic action.

The centre of the Minoan civilisation at this time was the island of Crete. There, from 1600 B.C., the Minoans had been building houses several storeys high, paved roads, and stone bridges. At this time, other people in Europe were still living in a primitive state.

At Knossos, Phaistos and other cities on Crete, the Minoans built magnificent palaces. But the Minoan civilisation came to an end suddenly at about the same time as the destruction of Thera. Was Crete, only eighty miles away, seriously affected by the eruption?

The palace at Knossos was first discovered by Sir Arthur Evans in 1900. From that date, some people have linked Crete and Atlantis. Here was an island with a splendid civilisation existing long before Plato. No doubt he had heard about it.

Today searchers for Atlantis are no longer looking for a lost continent. They are looking for pieces in a jigsaw—the pieces that Plato fitted together to invent Atlantis. It may well be that his idea for the destruction of Atlantis came from the destruction of Thera. This is only one piece in the jigsaw. There are a great many more left to find.

THE LOST EXPLORER

DEEP IN THE tropical jungle of the Amazon Basin, three white men had made camp. Their leader was an elderly man with a bald head under his bush hat. The other two were strapping youngsters, the taller standing six feet three inches. All three showed the signs of having been on the trail for some time. Their lightweight clothes looked worn, and their faces bore the marks of insect bites.

The three men were Lieutenant-Colonel P. H. Fawcett, his son, Jack, and Raleigh Rimmell. They were heading into an unexplored area of the jungle in search of a lost city believed to contain treasure. Colonel Fawcett called the city Z. Before setting out, he had said that he knew where Z was.

With the white men were two Indian guides. They were plainly nervous, fearful of going farther into the jungle. In the area ahead, they knew, lived tribes of savages. Fawcett sent the guides back from the camp with two horses which would have had trouble surviving in the thick forests ahead. They also carried a letter addressed to Fawcett's wife. In it the explorer said:

'We go on with eight animals, three saddle mules, four cargo mules and a leading animal which keeps the others together. Jack is fit and well, getting stronger every day, even though he suffers a bit from the insects. Raleigh I am anxious about. He still has one leg in a bandage but won't go back. I cannot hope to stand up to the journey better than Jack or Raleigh, but I had to do it. Years tell, in spite of the spirit of enthusiasm. I calculate to contact the Indians in about a week or ten days. You need have no fear of failure.'

This was the last message ever received from Colonel

Fawcett and his two companions. They were never seen again, except possibly by the savage tribes in the jungle. To this day, no one is sure what happened to them.

Colonel Fawcett was well fitted to lead the small expedition into the unexplored jungle. He had spent many years in the Amazon Basin and had often travelled in places where no white man had ever been before.

He went to South America for the first time in 1906 as a surveyor. He had been sent out by the Royal Geographical Society to carry out a difficult job. This was to survey the borders between Peru, Brazil and Bolivia, and mark them on the map. These borders ran through some of the wildest country in the world.

At this time, Fawcett was thirty-nine years old. He was a big man, standing over six feet tall. For twenty years he had been an officer in the Royal Regiment of Artillery serving in Ceylon, Malta and Hong Kong. As a young man he had been an all-round sportsman and he was still remarkably fit. He did not smoke and he never took alcoholic drinks.

Surveying the borders took Fawcett a year. It was a tough job. On landing in Peru, he went to Rio Blanco in the Andes. It was a startling journey for he travelled on the second-highest railway line in the world. In a distance of less than one hundred miles, the trains climb from sea level to a height of almost 16,000 feet.

To reach Bolivia, Fawcett travelled by ship, crossing Lake Titicaca. This is the highest navigable water in the world, 12,000 feet above sea level. The lake is one hundred and twenty-five miles long and sixty-nine miles wide.

Fawcett made his base in La Paz, the capital of Bolivia, and from there, at length, he set out to begin his work. The ground was covered with heavy snow as he left with one white companion and two Indian mule-drivers.

From the rocky heights of the mountains they climbed steadily down. Soon they reached the rain forests of the Amazon Basin. Mosquitoes, sand-flies and other insects plagued them in the steamy heat. They travelled by canoe along unmapped rivers, listening all the time for the sound of dangerous rapids. Once Fawcett's canoe was almost overturned by a giant anaconda snake. Fawcett shot it. It was about eighty feet long.

The days were burningly hot. Sometimes the temperature rose to over 100 degrees Fahrenheit in the shade. But the nights were always bitterly cold.

Fawcett passed through areas of the jungle where a

wide variety of animals lived—tapirs, ant-eaters, three-toed sloths, wild pigs, ocelots, pumas, jaguars, troops of chattering monkeys and many kinds of brightly-coloured birds. He passed along stretches of river where unpleasant creatures abounded—caymans, anacondas, sting-rays, electric eels and the fearsome piranha. The piranha are flesh-eating fish. Once excited by the smell of blood, they attack animals or humans in the water. They are said to be able to strip every particle of skin from a body within a few seconds.

Everywhere there were insects. There were flies of many shapes and sizes, and many of them were capable of inflicting bites that became poisoned. There were armies of driver ants, tens of thousands of them, systematically devouring everything in their path.

Several times, Fawcett narrowly escaped death. Once he was nearly drowned when his canoe overturned. On another occasion he found himself in the centre of a shower of arrows shot by hostile Indians.

In this region there were many savage tribes of Indians. Some of them were head-hunters. They used bows and arrows dipped in poison or fired poisoned darts from blowpipes.

After completing the survey, Fawcett went home to England. But in 1908 he was back in Brazil. Before leaving England he said, 'I love that green hell. It's fiendish grasp has captured me and I want to see it again.'

Back in Brazil, Fawcett set out once more into the jungle. He led a small expedition into the Matto Grosso, one of the last areas of Brazil to be explored. Fawcett's job was to trace the route of the River Verde. This was to be the border between Brazil and Bolivia.

Once again Fawcett overcame all the dangers of life in the unexplored jungle. He returned with excellent maps, and the officials in Bolivia were pleased with his work. He was offered more surveying jobs, and took them.

Fawcett spent six more years making maps of the Amazon Basin. Then World War One broke out in 1914, and he travelled home to rejoin the Army. The war ended in 1918, and, as soon as he could afterwards, Fawcett returned to Rio de Janeiro. He wanted to get back into the Amazon jungles. He was hoping one day to make an important discovery.

Fawcett believed that, somewhere in the forests, there must be traces of an old civilisation. From Indians he had met, he had heard many stories of ruins half-buried by the jungle. He used to say: 'It is certain that amazing ruins of ancient cities—ruins incomparably older than those in Egypt—exist in the far interior of Brazil. Whoever discovers them will add immensely to our knowledge of history. Perhaps even some descendants of unknown races like the Incas still live there.'

It was not, in those days, an improbable idea. The

Amazon Basin covers an area of two million square miles. It is equal to the area of all Europe. In 1918, only a small fraction of the area had been explored.

Nowadays aeroplanes fly over the jungles and large steamships sail 3,000 miles up the River Amazon right into the heart of Brazil. But away from the river the jungle is hard to penetrate. Even now, hundreds of thousands of square miles remain barely known to white men. In those days, over half a century ago, there were vast areas where no white man had ever been and others from which no white man had ever come out alive.

In 1920, Fawcett came across a document which excited him. It confirmed his belief in a lost civilisation. The document was a faded manuscript in the National Library of Brazil in Rio de Janeiro known by the number 512. It bore the title: Historic Account of a large, hidden City of great age, without inhabitants, which was discovered in the year 1753.

Manuscript number 512 contains the story of an expedition into the jungles of the River Amazon by a party of Portuguese adventurers led by Francisco Raposo. These adventurers were looking for gold and silver mines lost for two hundred years. Only one man had known where these mines were. He had been tortured for his secret by Portuguese officials, and died rather than reveal it.

Somehow, after many years of searching, the eighteenth century treasure-seekers found the lost mines on a plateau among jagged mountains. They also found, close by, an abandoned city, its streets littered with treasure.

Worn out but excited, Raposo and his men climbed down to the edge of the jungle, planning to return to the coast and come back with fresh supplies and equipment. From the banks of the Paraguassu River they sent an Indian runner on ahead. He was carrying a message for the Portuguese governor at the coastal town of

Bahia (Salvador). It was a report of the expedition, and today it is manuscript number 512.

That report was the last message ever received from Francisco Raposo and his men. After the Indian left them, they vanished in the jungle, and no trace of them has ever been discovered.

Fawcett called the city mentioned in Raposo's report 'Z', and told people he believed that it existed. 'Furthermore,' he said, 'I am going to find it.'

Later that year, Fawcett set off once more into the jungle. He had one companion with him, a young man named Felipe. They set out from Bahia (Salvador) and made their way westwards. At first they passed plantations and ranches carved out of the jungle. But, beyond the last plantation, they entered a thick, trackless and gloomy forest.

Fawcett hoped to collect information from Indians but he never saw one in the jungle. Yet, all the time, the two explorers must have been watched. Along the trail they saw plenty of signs that people had been about recently.

At one time rain began to fall in a continuous downpour. They plodded on, soaked to the skin.

Felipe grumbled a great deal of the time. Every day he complained of some new ailment. Unlike Fawcett, he was not used to life in the jungle.

It was a life to tax the hardiest of men. They were plagued by a variety of flies and ticks. At night they sometimes had to pull 60 to 80 ticks from their bodies. Each of these caused a slight, irritating wound. Yet the wounds must not be scratched. In such conditions, the slightest sore can easily become a festering wound.

Once Fawcett saw a spider the size of a sparrow sitting in its web. But what he disliked the most were the blood-sucking vampire bats. He said, 'In the mornings we woke to find our hammocks saturated with blood. Any parts of our bodies touching the mosquito nets or sticking out of them were attacked.'

Fawcett's journey with Felipe did not appear to be successful. Afterwards he made two more trips into the jungle alone and then he announced, 'I have learned a good deal. I am now sure I can find Z. But I want the right companions and the right organisation before I set out.'

As it turned out, it was five years before Fawcett set out to look for the lost city. For this expedition he chose two companions. They were his eldest son, Jack, aged twenty-two, and a schoolmate of Jack's, Raleigh Rimmell. The organisation of his expedition depended upon money, and Fawcett obtained this from certain scientific societies and from a news agency.

The story of the lost city of Z had been given a great deal of publicity in newspapers in the United States and Britain, and newspapers were prepared to pay well for the story of Fawcett's expedition.

Fawcett and his two companions left Cuyaba in April 1925. They set out with two Indian guides, two horses and eight mules. They intended to enter an area of unknown jungle between two rivers flowing from the south into the Amazon—the Xingu and the Araguaya.

On 29th May, the small party were more than three hundred and fifty miles to the north of Cuyaba. It was from here that Fawcett sent the Indians back with the horses and his last letter.

From this point, the mystery of what became of Colonel Fawcett begins.

Before setting out, Fawcett said that, if he found Z, he might stay there for some time. His expedition was well supplied with food and equipment, and it was two whole years before people became concerned about the three men. Then newspapers in Britain and the United States began to ask, in bold headlines,

WHERE IS COLONEL FAWCETT?

In 1927, a French explorer named Roger Courteville crossed South America from the Atlantic Ocean to the Pacific. In Peru he was asked if he had heard anything of Colonel Fawcett. He reported seeing a man who might have been Fawcett but his report was vague. It was not clear why he had not asked this strange man his name.

In 1928, a newspaper company in the United States sent out an expedition to look for Fawcett. They followed the route Fawcett's party had taken. A native chief told them about an old white man and two companions who had travelled in the jungle. He suggested that the three men had been killed by savages.

There was no definite evidence of what had happened to Fawcett. Yet the leader of the expedition, Commander George Dyott, stated: 'It is with the greatest regret that I have to announce Colonel Fawcett's fate. Both he, his son Jack and Raleigh Rimmell were killed by hostile Indians five days after crossing to the east of the Kuluene River some time during the month of July 1925. There is not the slightest doubt about this.'

But there was doubt. Dyott was asked for evidence and he could produce none. Many people believed that Fawcett might still be alive.

In 1930, a newspaper reporter set out to follow in Fawcett's footsteps. He himself was never heard of again.

Two years later, a Swiss trapper named Stephan Rattin, coming out of the jungle, told a strange story. He said that Fawcett was a prisoner of a savage tribe living on the Bomfin River. He had met, he said, an old man with a long, yellowish-white beard and long hair. This man said, 'I am an English colonel. Go to the English Consulate and ask them to tell Major Paget who has a coffee farm in São Paulo that I am a captive here.'

The man showed Rattin a gold locket he was wearing around his neck. Inside was the photograph of a lady in a large hat with two children. Rattin described the old man as being about sixty-five years old, well built and about five feet eleven inches tall. His eyes, he said, were bright blue.

Rattin's story was examined. It was true that Fawcett had a great friend named Sir Ralph Paget. But Fawcett's beard would have been grey and he had been bald for many years. He was well over six feet tall and his eyes were grey, not blue. Whoever the man was Rattin had met, that man did not appear to be Colonel Fawcett.

As time went by, contact with the savage tribes in the jungle improved slightly. From time to time stories were heard of an old white man living in the jungle. The legend persisted that somehow Fawcett had survived and was living with primitive Indians. Other expeditions set out in search of him. But they found no conclusive evidence.

In 1933, the Royal Geographical Society in London was sent a compass found near a camp of Indians in the Matto Grosso. It was one that had been supplied to Colonel Fawcett. But it seemed probable that he had lost it there on his expedition with Felipe in 1920.

That same year, an expedition visiting the Kuluene River heard a strange story. A traveller in the area had met an Indian woman who spoke some words of Portuguese. She told him that white men had lived for years with a nearby tribe of savages. There were three of them, and they had arrived about ten years earlier. One man was old, another was his son, and the third was 'a white man of greater age'. The men were treated well, but they were not allowed to leave. No trace of these three men was ever found. Could they have been Fawcett and his two young companions? How could it have happened that Raleigh Rimmell should appear to be older than Colonel Fawcett?

Right up to the start of World War Two in 1939, the mystery of Colonel Fawcett's disappearance was often referred to in newspapers. When the war ended in 1945, the mystery still claimed attention.

In 1950, Colonel Fawcett's younger son, Brian, visited Brazil. In an effort to solve the mystery he followed his father's trail into the jungle. From an aeroplane he surveyed the area where his father had vanished. He returned with the mystery still unsolved. He said, 'I believe there is a chance that my brother Jack may still be alive somewhere in the jungle.'

In 1950 also, Señor Orlando Vilas Boas, one of the foremost experts on the Amazon Basin, was at the bedside of a dying Indian chief. This man made a confession. He said that, in a quarrel, he clubbed Fawcett and his two young companions to death.

Many people refused to accept this. In his account of the quarrel, the chief said that Fawcett had first slapped his face. People who knew the lost explorer said that this did not make sense. It was not the way Fawcett would ever behave.

The new chief was asked to show where the bodies were buried. He said that the two young men's bodies had been thrown in the river and carried away. But he knew where Fawcett's grave was.

The grave was dug up, and the bones taken out. They were flown to London and there experts at the Royal Anthropological Institute examined them. Then they gave their opinion. The bones could not belong to Colonel Fawcett. They belonged to someone much shorter than he was. Indeed, they were probably not the bones of a white man at all.

In 1962, thirty-seven years after Colonel Fawcett disappeared, a programme on B.B.C. television recalled the mystery. By their own firesides in England, people were able to follow, through the camera's eye, the route that Fawcett had probably taken.

But they did not hear the solution to the mystery.

To this day, no one knows what that is.

THE MAN IN THE IRON MASK

THE BASTILLE WAS a grim prison fortress standing in the centre of Paris. In it were kept important criminals and enemies of the King of France. There, one afternoon in September, 1698, a prisoner arrived in the care of the new governor, Monsieur de Saint-Mars.

The prisoner was a tall man and neatly dressed but what he looked like no one knows to this day. His face was hidden by an iron mask.

Who was the Man in the Iron Mask? This is one of the best kept secrets of history. For over two centuries people have been trying to work out the answer. His story has been told in books, plays and films. Different solutions have been given to the mystery. But no one knows which solution is correct.

In 1669, Monsieur de Saint-Mars was in charge of a prison at Pignerol which included several important prisoners. In 1681 he was sent to be governor of the Fortress of Exiles, thirty miles from Pignerol. He took two prisoners with him.

Six years later, Saint-Mars was placed in charge of the prison fortress on the island of St. Marguerite in the Bay of Cannes. He took one or perhaps two prisoners with him, and the face of one was hidden by a mask.

Exactly what that mask looked like no one knows. It hid enough of the prisoner's face to stop anyone recognising him. Probably it was locked around the neck.

One of the jailers at the Bastille kept a diary and, in this, he later referred to a mask of velvet. Perhaps the 'iron mask' was a frame of iron with velvet inside it. The velvet would wear out but it could be replaced from time to time. The iron frame would be needed so

that it could be locked on. It was obviously important to stop the prisoner from taking the mask off himself.

Saint-Mars and the Man in the Iron Mask remained on St. Marguerite for eleven years. In that time, according to some accounts, one curious incident took place. One day a local fisherman, fishing close by the walls of the prison, found something gleaming among the fish and weeds in his net. It was a silver plate, and scratched on its bright surface were some markings.

The fisherman recognised the marks as writing. He also saw a crest on the plate. It was the fleur-de-lys—the sign of the kings of France. At once he hurried to the prison with the plate.

The prison guard inspected the plate and told the fisherman not to go away. After some delay he was taken to see Monsieur de Saint-Mars. He stood nervously as the governor of St. Marguerite Prison looked closely at the scratches on the silver plate.

At last Saint-Mars spoke. 'Have you read the message on this plate?' he asked.

The fisherman shook his head. 'No, sir,' he replied. 'I am ashamed to say that I cannot read.'

Saint-Mars fixed him with a keen stare. 'Have you shown the plate to anyone else?' he demanded.

Again the fisherman shook his head. 'I have shown it to no one,' he said. 'I landed my catch and then I came straight here. I had seen the King's sign on the plate. I guessed it must have come from the fortress.'

'You have done well,' said Saint-Mars. He handed the

man a gold piece. 'This is your reward. But you must forget that you ever saw this plate. Just remember that you are a lucky man.'

'I am indeed lucky,' said the man. He smiled down at the gold coin in his brown hand.

Saint-Mars shook his head. 'I don't mean that. I mean that you are lucky *because you cannot read.*'

It seems plain that the message on the silver plate was written by the Man in the Iron Mask. Possibly it contained his name. If the fisherman had read the message, he would have known the secret of the Man in the Iron Mask. That is how he was lucky. Otherwise he would have known too much to be allowed to go free.

At the Bastille, the Man in the Iron Mask was placed in a room in one of the towers. In his diary the jailer, Etienne de Jonca, tells how he prepared a room for the prisoner. It is clear that the prisoner was treated well. He was looked after and waited upon by a servant and Saint-Mars always showed an interest in him.

The Man in the Iron Mask was allowed to attend Mass in the Bastille. On Sunday, 18th November, 1703, he fell ill after getting back to his room. Next night, with a priest at his side, he died suddenly.

No time was wasted in disposing of the body. The prisoner was buried next day in the graveyard of the near-by parish church of St. Paul. There were no mourners.

A name had to be entered into the church's burial register and one was. The name was Marchioly.

The dead man's age was given as forty-five years. This is clearly false. If he was a prisoner at Pignerol thirty-four years earlier he must have been a great deal older.

Meantime, back in the Bastille, the prisoner's room was stripped of its possessions. Every possible piece of furniture was burned and metal objects were melted down. The walls of the room were scraped. The floor was taken up and burned, the ceiling pulled down and crushed. No sign remained of the Man in the Iron Mask, no chance of an inscription or carving providing a clue to who he was.

It is believed that Saint-Mars knew who the prisoner was. It was said that, in his early years in prison, he did not wear a mask. Yet is this probable? If an old prisoner were placed in a mask to hide who he was, every guard in the prison would know his secret. Isn't it more likely that the prisoner wore his mask from the time he first entered prison?

It is clear that King Louis XIV knew about the masked prisoner and wanted his secret to be kept. When Saint-Mars was going to the Bastille, he received a message. It said: 'The King approves your leaving the island of St. Marguerite to come to the Bastille with your ancient prisoner, taking all precautions to prevent his being seen or recognised by anyone.'

It is said that Saint-Mars stopped on the way to Paris at his own home, a chateau near Villeneuve. He and his masked prisoner ate dinner together that night, and Saint-Mars had two pistols on the table beside his plate. In later years the servants recalled the Man in the Iron Mask. 'He was tall,' they said. 'And his hair was quite white.'

Whatever Saint-Mars knew about his prisoner, he took the secret to the grave with him and left the world a mystery.

On 14th July, 1789, the Bastille was attacked by a mob of people and the French Revolution began. The hated prison was captured and pulled down. It is said that, at this time, official documents were saved and later inspected for information about the Man in the Iron Mask. It seems that even Napoleon tried to find out who he was. But the documents were of no help. The mystery remained.

The famous French author, Alexandre Dumas (1802–70), put forward one solution in a novel called

The Man in the Iron Mask. In this story, Louis XIII was said to have been the father of twin sons. He was afraid that the two might grow up to be rivals for the throne of France. So he sent the younger twin away to be looked after by a governess.

In 1658, the elder son, now King Louis XIV, arranged for his brother to be put in prison for life. The twins looked very much alike. Someone seeing the younger son's face might guess he was related to Louis. So Louis ordered his face to be hidden forever with the iron mask.

In modern times many experts have studied the mystery. They have not agreed upon a solution but they agree on one point. Dumas's story provides a most unlikely solution. There is no evidence to support it.

According to one early explanation, the Man in the Iron Mask was an Englishman, the Duke of Monmouth. Monmouth was a son of King Charles II of England. In 1685 he led a rebellion against his uncle, King James II, and was defeated at the Battle of Sedgemoor in Somerset.

Monmouth was tried and convicted of treason and executed at the Tower of London—or was he? Some said that another man was beheaded in his place. King James had made a secret agreement with King Louis XIV of France to save his nephew. Monmouth was released and travelled in secret to France but there he had to be kept prisoner with his face hidden.

In England a woman named Lady Wentworth said that she had looked into Monmouth's coffin and been shocked. The severed head was certainly not Monmouth's, she insisted. But it is agreed today that Monmouth was almost certainly not the Man in the Iron Mask.

Today many experts believe that the Man in the Iron Mask was an Italian count named Ercole Mattioli, an official of the Duke of Mantua. Mattioli had the job of selling a fortress to King Louis XIV. It stood on the borders of Italy and France, and it was to cost one hundred thousand crowns.

At this time, Italy was not a single country like it is today. It was made up of lots of small states, each with its own ruler. But King Louis discovered that the Duke of Mantua was trying to band a group of states together. Then they might be more powerful than France.

The Duke's plan was being put into practice by Mattioli. He was travelling from place to place carrying messages between the different rulers. At the same time, he was pretending that he and the Duke were friends of France, and offering the castle for sale.

On discovering Count Mattioli's secret, King Louis was furious. At once he sent agents to kidnap Mattioli. They travelled into Italy and found him in Turin at the palace of the Duke of Savoy. They waited their chance and then seized him and drove post-haste back over the border into France. There Louis had Mattioli put in prison for life and, to hide who he was, instructed that he should be kept masked for ever. If Mattioli had been kept in prison openly, there would have been trouble with the Duke of Mantua.

Other people believe that the masked prisoner was a man named Eustache Dauger. Old documents show that a prisoner named Dauger (or Douger, as the name is sometimes spelled) arrived at the prison at Pignerol in August 1669. He had been arrested in Dunkirk by an agent of King Louis XIV on the direct orders of the King, and he was never tried for any crime.

Meantime, Saint-Mars had received a letter from the Minister of War, the Marquis de Louvois. This letter warned him that a special prisoner was on his way to Pignerol and that this man must be closely guarded at all times. Louvois said: 'It is of the utmost importance that he should in no way give information about himself nor send letters to anyone at all.'

Saint-Mars took his orders seriously. He warned Dauger that he must never speak to anyone in the prison about anything except things he needed. 'If you do,' he said, 'I shall run you through with my sword.'

Inside the fortress at Pignerol there were other important prisoners of state and, at first, Saint-Mars made sure that they did not meet Dauger. But in 1672 he made a curious request to the Marquis de Louvois.

Among the prisoners at Pignerol was Monsieur Nicolas Fouquet, a minister of the King who had fallen into disgrace. Fouquet was, at this time, known as France's most important prisoner. He was allowed a servant in prison but Saint-Mars was unable to find a good one. So he made his request. He asked Louvois if Dauger could act as servant to Fouquet, and the answer was 'Yes.'

At this stage, clearly, Dauger was not masked, and Saint-Mars was warned that another prisoner must never see his face. This was the Comte de Lauzun, sometime captain in the King's Guard. Presumably Lauzun might have recognised Dauger. This meant that, on some occasion, their paths had crossed. On the other hand, the prisoner must have been unknown to Fouquet. These facts add a little more to our knowledge of the man called Dauger.

Strangely enough, Lauzun was soon seeing Dauger unknown to Saint-Mars. By removing some bars from a chimney, he made a secret entry into Fouquet's room, and the two men met there often—sometimes, no doubt, when Dauger was present.

In 1680, Fouquet died, and afterwards Dauger was locked in a room of one of the towers. Lauzun was told, 'The man named Dauger has been released.' Whether he believed this is not known. He himself was set free two years later and soon afterwards went to see King Louis XIV. He is not known to have ever spoken of Dauger after leaving Pignerol.

From Pignerol, Saint-Mars moved to the Fortress of Exiles in 1681, and it is believed that he took Dauger with him. Six years later, he was moved to command the prison on St. Marguerite. Again he took Dauger with him and it is possible that, at this point, Dauger was masked.

It seems that Ercole Mattioli was one of the prisoners on St. Marguerite, too. Some people say that he died there in 1696. At one time Mattioli was also at Pignerol. This explains why some people believe that he was the Man in the Iron Mask. For the Man in the Iron Mask is thought to have gone from prison to prison with Saint-Mars.

From the time Saint-Mars moved from Pignerol, he never referred to Dauger by name. In letters to and from Louvois, he referred to the 'ancient prisoner'. Again there is the possibility of confusion with Mattioli.

The 'ancient prisoner' was certainly masked when he reached the Bastille in 1698 and died there five years later. Was he Mattioli? Was he Dauger?

If we accept that Mattioli died on St. Marguerite in 1696, then the Man in the Iron Mask was Dauger. But who was Dauger? When he was sent to Pignerol it was said that he was a valet. That word, in those days, meant a servant or secretary. He appeared to be a well educated person and he was a Catholic; we know this because he used to go to Mass in prison. At the time of his death he must have been around sixty years old.

For many long years, people searched records in France to try to find someone named Dauger born about 1640. In 1930, such a person was discovered— Eustache d'Auger or Dauger born in 1637. This Dauger was the son of a captain in Cardinal Richelieu's Musketeers, and he and his wife were friends of King Louis XIII.

Eustache and his brothers grew up in contact with

the Court of France and they knew the young prince who became Louis XIV. As a young man, Dauger became an officer in the King's Guard. By the age of twenty-one he had fought in a number of campaigns and three of his brothers had been killed.

Dauger was a dashing, fun-loving young man, and he took part in a number of wild escapades. Once he and a companion killed a drunken page on the staircase of the royal palace. Yet it was not for this that he was put in prison.

In 1668, he was living with his brother, Louis, in Paris. That year Louis was involved in a duel with a member of the King's Court. For this he was sent to the Bastille. He was released after some months and, by that time, Eustache had vanished.

Unless he was the prisoner Dauger, no trace of him exists after that date. There is no record of his death.

Perhaps then this Eustache Dauger, sometime officer in the King's Guard, was the Man in the Iron Mask. It fits in with the fact that he was not supposed to be seen at Pignerol by the Comte de Lauzun, a former captain in the King's Guard. But the question remains: Why was he put in prison?

The answer to that question is still a mystery. One explanation is that he looked like King Louis XIV. Perhaps, say some people, he offended the King by pretending to be him on some occasion. The fun-loving Eustache Dauger might play such a trick if, indeed, he did look like the King.

This explanation leaves two large questions open: 1. If Dauger was put in prison because he looked like Louis XIV, why was he not made to wear a mask from the start of his imprisonment? 2. Why didn't his parents, or his brothers and sisters (there were six sons and three daughters in the family) protest for his freedom?

This second question, of course, applies to anyone

who was the Man with the Iron Mask. Why were there no protests when he was arrested? Why was there no talk among his friends and relatives?

As to Dauger, the whole idea of tracing him may be a mistaken one. Can we be sure that the prisoner's name was really Dauger? In such a secret operation, wouldn't a false name be used?

So we think again of Count Ercole Mattioli, agent of the Duke of Mantua. Mattioli was a secret agent from a foreign country. In Italy his disappearance would have been noted but it would not have been completely unexpected. A secret agent was always in danger of being wiped out.

King Louis would not want it known that he was holding Mattioli as a prisoner. He would not want to have trouble with the Italian states. So he might have Mattioli's face hidden by a mask from the time of his imprisonment. In the case of Dauger, the idea of putting a mask on a known prisoner seems odd, anyway.

Perhaps Mattioli did not die in the prison on St. Marguerite in 1696. Perhaps Dauger died and Mattioli did not die until 1703—in the Bastille, to be buried at the church of St. Paul, his strange Italian name carelessly written down as Marchioly.

THE FROGMAN WHO VANISHED

On Monday, 30th April, 1956, headlines like the following appeared on the front pages of newspapers in Britain.

MISSING FROGMAN MYSTERY

Under the headlines the story was told. The main part of it was in the form of a statement from the Admiralty about Lieutenant-Commander Lionel Crabb, O.B.E., G.M., R.N.V.R. It said: 'He is presumed to be dead as a result of trials with certain underwater apparatus. The location was in Stokes Bay, and it is nine days since the accident.'

There was really nothing sensational in the statement from the Admiralty. Why, then, did the newspapers give it such an important place? The story told that, too. At this time, the two leaders of the Soviet Union, Nikita Krushchev and Marshal Nikolai Bulganin, were visiting Britain. They had travelled by sea, and a flotilla of Soviet warships was anchored in the harbour at Portsmouth, not far from Stokes Bay.

In World War Two, Britain and the Soviet Union were allies. But, from the end of the war in 1945, the two nations drifted apart. Soon they were no longer friends and many people said that there was a 'cold war' between them. Then Krushchev and Bulganin decided to make a friendly visit to Britain. 'This is good news,' said the experts in the newspapers. 'It means that the 'cold war" is coming to an end.'

Now the same experts were worried about Commander Crabb. 'What was he doing in Portsmouth harbour?' they asked. 'It cannot help friendship with the Soviet Union if he was spying on the Soviet warships.'

Newspaper reporters hurried to Portsmouth to try to find out more about what had happened. They were ready to interview anyone who knew Commander Crabb. They wanted to piece together the story of the missing frogman's last few days.

Crabb was well known in Portsmouth. He was a wartime hero twice decorated for his underwater exploits with the Royal Navy. The newspaper reporters found that he had been seen in Portsmouth with a mysterious American known as Matthew Smith. The two men were believed to have stayed at the Sallyport Hotel but this fact could not be proved. A man said to be a detective had visited the hotel and torn four pages out of the hotel register. The four pages included the day when Commander Crabb and Smith probably signed the register.

By this time, a number of rumours were circulating about Crabb's last dive.

1. Crabb was making an experimental dive and he was seen from the Sovict cruiser Ordzhonikidze. The Russians thought he was going to damage their ship and killed him. His body was found floating in the harbour and buried in secret with full military honours.

2. Crabb was inspecting the hull of the Ordzhonikidze. He was seen from the cruiser and captured. He was being taken back to Russia as a prisoner.

3. Crabb was photographing the hull of the cruiser with a portable television camera. He became entangled in the cable and drowned.

4. Crabb had dived near the cruiser in order to obtain publicity for himself. He was writing the story of

his adventures, and this would help to make him famous. Something went wrong and somehow he was killed.

It was known, by this time, that, in 1955, Commander Crabb had carried out a secret mission against the Soviet cruiser Sverdlov. She visited Britain that autumn and the frogman went down and carried out a close inspection of her hull. He was looking for signs of secret equipment and he brought back a report of everything he saw.

According to one rumour, Crabb had taken a geiger counter with him on his last dive in Portsmouth harbour. He was supposed to be trying to find out if there was an atom bomb aboard the Ordzhonikidze! If he had been on a secret mission, it was agreed, this was the Soviet ship he was most likely to have been spying on. It was probably the fastest and most manoeuvrable vessel of its kind in the world.

The Soviet Union did not ignore the rumours about Commander Crabb. On 4th May, they sent a note to the British Foreign Office. It stated: 'During the stay of Soviet warships in Portsmouth at 7.30 a.m. on April 19 seamen on board a Soviet ship observed a frogman floating between the Soviet destroyers.' According to the note, the commander of the Soviet flotilla had asked the Royal Navy at Portsmouth about this, and had been told that there had been no British frogmen in the harbour at that time. But the statement from the Admiralty about Commander Crabb's death showed that this was not true. The note asked, politely, for 'an explanation of this matter.'

Five days later, the matter was raised in Parliament. An M.P. asked, 'What were the circumstances under which Commander Crabb disappeared?' The Prime Minister, Sir Anthony Eden, replied: 'It would not be in the public interest to disclose the circumstances in which Commander Crabb met his death.' At this there were loud cries of protest from the M.P.s in Parliament. 'Oh! Oh!' Sir Anthony went on to say that whatever had happened at Portsmouth had happened without anyone in the Government knowing anything about it.

The Prime Minister's words were printed in the newspapers, and most people had their own idea of what they meant. 'It's pretty obvious now, isn't it?' they said. 'Crabb was spying on the Russian cruiser but no one wants to take the blame for it.'

At the same time, the Government replied to the Soviet note about the frogman seen at Portsmouth. They said that Commander Crabb had been diving in Portsmouth harbour at the time the frogman was seen and that, presumably, the man seen from the Soviet ship was Crabb. The reply ended: 'His presence in the vicinity of the destroyers occurred without any permission whatever, and Her Majesty's Government express their regret for the incident.'

On 14th May, the Commander Crabb Affair, as it was being called, was mentioned in Parliament once more. Again Sir Anthony Eden refused to say any more on the subject. There was talk about whether the British Secret Service had anything to do with his dive but Sir Anthony said he was not prepared to discuss this. He said, firmly, 'We are dealing with circumstances in which no government in any country would say more than I am prepared to say.' Again people thought that this meant that Crabb was spying on the Russians.

In the weeks and months that followed, the Commander Crabb Affair gradually became forgotten. But in May 1957 it was in the news again. That month a newspaper in London contained the following statement. It was said to have been made by someone in an official position. 'We are satisfied that Commander Crabb did not die when he went into the water at Portsmouth near the Russian ships. We have good reason to believe that he was taken aboard one of the ships and is now held in Russia.'

The full story of the Commander Crabb Affair was told again in the newspapers. This time it ended with a new question: Is Commander Crabb alive?

The question was still being asked on 9th June, 1957. That day Mr. John Randall was out fishing off Pilsey Island, a sandbank at the mouth of Chichester Harbour. There he saw a body floating in the sea. It was dressed in a frogman's suit.

There were two men with Mr. Randall and the three of them pulled the body into their boat. They took it back to the shore and handed it over to the Police.

The body was taken to a hospital in Chichester and Dr. Donald King examined it. He was unable to discover the cause of death. Also he said it was not going to be easy to identify the body. The head was missing and so were the hands.

Already people were thinking about Commander Crabb, and his ex-wife, Mrs. Margaret Crabb, was sent for. She inspected the body and could not identify it. She told the Police that Crabb had deformed toes, and the toes on the body did not appear to be deformed. Yet Superintendent S. L. Simmonds of Chichester Police said that the body was probably Commander Crabb's. The currents in the sea would tend to carry a body from Portsmouth in the direction of Chichester, he said.

On 11th June, an inquest on the 'unidentified man' was begun at Winchester. It was continued on 26th June and a number of people who had known Commander Crabb were called to give evidence.

Dr. King said that the body belonged to a man about five feet six inches tall. That was the height of Commander Crabb.

He said that the body had been in the sea for at least six months and might have been in the sea for fourteen months. It was fourteen months since Commander Crabb disappeared in Portsmouth harbour.

There was a scar on the left knee of the dead man. Mr. Sydney James Knowles said that Commander Crabb had such a scar. Mr. Knowles had served with him in World War Two on underwater operations. He said that Crabb had been cut by barbed wire in an operation in Leghorn harbour in Italy in 1945. The injury had left him with the scar.

The body had been dressed in an unusual type of frogman's suit. It had a neck seal instead of a hood. A maker of swimming suits was in court to give evidence. He said that the suit was like suits he had supplied to Crabb.

At length, the coroner gave his verdict: Death from unknown causes. Then he added: 'Looking at the evidence in the case, I am quite satisfied that the body is that of Commander Crabb.'

Commander Crabb's mother, Mrs. Beatrice Crabb, sent a solicitor to the inquest. Afterwards he said: 'Everything indicates that this very gallant gentleman died, as he had lived, in the service of his country.'

The Admiralty were asked to comment. A spokesman said: 'The Admiralty can add nothing to its original statement or to the statement of the Prime Minister.'

On Friday, 5th July, 1957, the body believed to be Commander Crabb's was buried at Milton Cemetery, Portsmouth. On the face of it, the Commander Crabb Affair was over. He had dived in Portsmouth harbour on 19th April, 1956, for a secret reason. The secret reason could be guessed at—an inspection of the hull of the Soviet cruiser Ordzhonikidze. On the dive he had been killed, either by accident or by a secret device on the cruiser. But there were still parts of the story missing. For example: Who sent Crabb on his secret mission? Some newspapers tried to fill in the missing parts of the story. They told and retold the story of Crabb's last dive.

It was said that the mysterious American, Matthew

Smith, had given him his orders to dive under the Ordzhonikidze. 'Those orders could not have come from the Admiralty,' said the experts. 'They would not use an American for such a job.' This seemed to leave two possibilities—(a) the British Secret Service and (b) the United States Secret Service. But there was a third possibility. This was explored thoroughly in a book by J. Bernard Hutton, *Commander Crabb Is Alive*.

Mr. Hutton said that Matthew Smith was a double agent. He pretended to work for the U.S. Secret Service and the Admiralty but, in fact, he was a Soviet spy. The mission he was sent on was planned with one object: the capture of Commander Crabb.

Crabb was not only a greatly experienced and highly skilled frogman. He was also an expert on every type of explosive and on underwater warfare. His knowledge and his skill would be very valuable to the Russians.

Smith stayed with Crabb at the Sallyport Hotel. They

were seen about Portsmouth together. At the docks
Smith met a Soviet agent in secret and told him that
the dive was on.

Commander Crabb entered the water of Portsmouth
Harbour at seven o'clock in the morning of 19th April.
He swam under water towards the Ordzhonikidze.
Soviet divers were waiting for him. They overpowered
him and took him aboard the cruiser through an under-
water air lock.

Later that day, Matthew Smith left Portsmouth. He
had received word from the Ordzhonikidze. He knew
that Crabb was a prisoner aboard.

Soon the Soviet flotilla was on its way back to Russia.
According to Hutton, Crabb was put ashore by helicopter. At least, a Danish destroyer saw two men taken off
the Ordzhonikidze by helicopter and one of them was
leading the other. Some time before this the destroyer
had picked up two Soviet wireless messages in code.

Later they were decoded. Both referred to a prisoner being taken off the Ordzhonikidze.

In Moscow, Crabb was kept in prison for a time. He was questioned over and over again and accused of spying for the U.S. Secret Service. He refused to admit this and one questioner said to him, bluntly, 'You know that you can be put to death as a spy.' In the end, though, he was offered a place in the Soviet Navy as an officer. He accepted and was given a new name, Lev Lvovich Korablov, and at once began to learn to speak Russian. Hutton's book contains photographs said to show Crabb in the Russian Navy.

If this is true, whose body was buried as Crabb at Portsmouth? Hutton explains this, too. A body of about the same height as Crabb and dressed in his diving gear was kept by the Russians in sea water for months. The head and hands were removed. The body was dropped in the English Channel near Chichester in June 1957 by a Soviet submarine.

After the body was found, an interesting fact had come to light. Some days earlier, three Soviet submarines had passed through the English Channel.

Occasionally, after 1957, reports appeared in British newspapers under the heading

CRABB IN RUSSIA?

Such reports told vague stories. Someone had seen a person who might have been Commander Crabb. Hutton's book contains many reports of Crabb's supposed activities in the Soviet Union. Yet the mystery remains. Who knows what really happened to Commander Crabb? What was he doing in Portsmouth Harbour that day in April 1956?

Does his body lie in a grave at Milton Cemetery, Portsmouth?

Or is he still today alive and well in the Soviet Union?

THE BOOK OF EXPERIMENTS
by Leonard de Vries   30p

552 54020 X

Would you like to become an inventor? This book will show you
how. Would you like to experience the adventure of scientific
discovery in your own home? This book offers 150 such experiments which can be done safely and at little or no cost—for
example, with nails you can make either a piano or an electric
motor. Many equally amazing discoveries await the reader of this
book.

ALL ABOUT WEATHER
by John Hulbert   30p

552 54040 4   Carousel Non-Fiction

Weather is taken for granted as an inescapable and often dreary
feature of everyday life. But weather is one of the most fascinat-
ing subjects for study, as it has a tremendous influence on our
whole pattern of existence—the house we live in, the clothes we
wear, the food we eat, the way we behave.

ALL ABOUT WEATHER explains the physical basis of weather
and tells exactly why it works as it does in different regions. It
examines every aspect of weather—from hurricanes to fog and
snow, and looks at the mysteries of weather forecasting; the
meteorologist's equipment, his methods and his problems; and
simple experiments and research that can be done.

DISCOVERERS AND ADVENTURERS
by R. J. Unstead   30p

552 54031 5   Carousel Non-Fiction

R. J. Unstead has chosen some of the most exciting and intriguing
discoverers and adventurers and tells their stories. Among the
people he has written about are—John Cabot, who tried to find
the North-West Passage, but failed; Lady Jane Grey, who was
Queen of England for only nine days; John Smith, who was the
real founder of Virginia; and William Dampier, the famous
buccaneer.

EVERYDAY LIFE IN EARLY IMPERIAL CHINA
by Michael Loewe   35p

552 54043 9   Carousel Non-Fiction

What was it like to live in Imperial China during her first four centuries of greatness 2000 years ago? How did the emperor rule over 50 million inhabitants in over 100 administrative divisions? Michael Lowe paints a full and vivid picture of the Han period (202 B.C.–A.D. 220). He describes the life of the peasants working the land, as well as the inhabitants of the towns—the rich, the tradesmen and artisans, the courtiers and officials, and the beggars and criminals. He examines their position in society, their work, their stints of government service—either as statutory labourers or in the army, their religious practices, and the elaborate hierarchy of institutions and civil servants who enforced the decisions of the imperial government.

OPERATION SIPPACIK
by Rumer Godden   20p

552 52009 8   Carousel Fiction

It took a war to prove the heroism of Sippacik, when she was sent out on a vital mission for the 27th Battery, Royal Artillery, stationed in Cyprus. 'Seytan'—devil—was the name Arif Ali had given her, but to her owner Sippacik was the cleverest donkey in Cyprus. She had to be, she was about to face the enemy. This is her true story.

All these books are available at your bookshop or can be ordered direct from Transworld Publishers Ltd., Cash Sales Dept., P.O. Box 11, Falmouth, Cornwall.

Please send full name and address together with cheque or postal order—no currency, and allow 7p per book to cover the cost of postage and packing.

If you would like to receive a newsletter telling you about our new children's books, send your name and address to Gillian Osband, Transworld Publishers Ltd., 57/59 Uxbridge Road, Ealing, London, W5, and mention 'CHILDREN'S NEWSLETTER'.